Miami Marlins 2021

A Baseball Companion

Edited by Steven Goldman and Bret Sayre

Baseball Prospectus

Craig Brown, Associate Editor
Robert Au, Harry Pavlidis and Amy Pircher, Statistics Editors

Copyright © 2021 by DIY Baseball, LLC.
All rights reserved

This book or any part thereof may not be reproduced or transmitted in any form or by any means, electronic or mechanical, including photocopying, recording, or by any information storage and retrieval system, without permission in writing from the publisher.

Limit of Liability/Disclaimer of Warranty: While the publisher and the author have used their best efforts in preparing this book, they make no representations or warranties with respect to the accuracy or completeness of the contents of this book and specifically disclaim any implied warranties of merchantability or fitness for a particular purpose. No warranty may be created or extended by sales representatives or written sales materials. The advice and strategies contained herein may not be suitable for your situation. You should consult with a professional where appropriate. Neither the publisher nor the author shall be liable for any loss of profit or any other commercial damages, including but not limited to special, incidental, consequential, or other damages.

Library of Congress Cataloging-in-Publication Data:
paperback
ISBN-13: 978-1-950716-53-1

Project Credits
Cover Design: Ginny Searle
Interior Design and Production: Amy Pircher, Robert Au
Layout: Amy Pircher, Robert Au

Baseball icon courtesy of Uberux, from https://www.shareicon.net/author/uberux

Ballpark diagram courtesy of Lou Spirito/THIRTY81 Project, https://thirty81project.com/

Manufactured in the United States of America
10 9 8 7 6 5 4 3 2 1

Table of Contents

Statistical Introduction v

Part 1: Team Analysis
Performance Graphs 3
2020 Team Performance 4
2021 Team Projections 5
Team Personnel 6
Marlins Park Stats 7
Marlins Team Analysis 9

Part 2: Player Analysis
Marlins Player Analysis 16
Marlins Prospects 89

Part 3: Featured Articles
Marlins All-Time Top 10 Players 103
    by Matthew Trueblood

A Taxonomy of 2020 Abnormalities 109
    by Rob Mains

Tranches of WAR 115
    by Russell A. Carleton

Secondhand Sport 121
    by Patrick Dubuque

Steve Dalkowski Dreaming 125
    by Steven Goldman

A Reward For A Functioning Society 129
    by Cory Frontin and Craig Goldstein

Index of Names 133

Statistical Introduction

Sports are, fundamentally, a blend of athletic endeavor and storytelling. Baseball, like any other sport, tells its stories in so many ways: in the arc of a game from the stands or a season from the box scores, in photos, or even in numbers. At Baseball Prospectus, we understand that statistics don't replace observation or any of baseball's stories, but complement everything else that makes the game so much fun.

What stats help us with is with patterns and precision, variance and value. This book can help you learn things you may not see from watching a game or hundred, whether it's the path of a career over time or the breadth of the entire MLB. We'd also never ask you to choose between our numbers and the experience of viewing a game from the cheap seats or the comfort of your home; our publication combines running the numbers with observations and wisdom from some of the brightest minds we can find. But if you *do* want to learn more about the numbers beyond what's on the backs of player jerseys, let us help explain.

Offense

We've revised our methodology for determining batting value. Long-time readers of the book will notice that we've retired True Average in favor of a new metric: Deserved Runs Created Plus (DRC+). Developed by Jonathan Judge and our stats team, this statistic measures everything a player does at the plate–reaching base, hitting for power, making outs, and moving runners over–and puts it on a scale where 100 equals league-average performance. A DRC+ of 150 is terrific, a DRC+ of 100 is average and a DRC+ of 75 means you better be an excellent defender.

DRC+ also does a better job than any of our previous metrics in taking contextual factors into account. The model adjusts for how the park affects performance, but also for things like the talent of the opposing pitcher, value of different types of batted-ball events, league, temperature and other factors. It's able to describe a player's expected offensive contribution than any other statistic we've found over the years, and also does a better job of predicting future performance as well.

The other aspect of run-scoring is baserunning, which we quantify using Baserunning Runs. BRR not only records the value of stolen bases (or getting caught in the act), but also accounts for all the stuff that doesn't show up on the back of a baseball card: a runner's ability to go first to third on a single, or advance on a fly ball.

Defense

Where offensive value is *relatively* easy to identify and understand, defensive value is … not. Over the past dozen years, the sabermetric community has focused mostly on stats based on zone data: a real-live human person records the type of batted ball and estimated landing location, and models are created that give expected outs. From there, you can compare fielders' actual outs to those expected ones. Simple, right?

Unfortunately, zone data has two major issues. First, zone data is recorded by commercial data providers who keep the raw data private unless you pay for it. (All the statistics we build in this book and on our website use public data as inputs.) That hurts our ability to test assumptions or duplicate results. Second, over the years it has become apparent that there's quite a bit of "noise" in zone-based fielding analysis. Sometimes the conclusions drawn from zone data don't hold up to scrutiny, and sometimes the different data provided by different providers don't look anything alike, giving wildly different results. Sometimes the hard-working professional stringers or scorers might unknowingly inflict unconscious bias into the mix: for example good fielders will often be credited with more expected outs despite the data, and ballparks with high press boxes tend to score more line drives than ones with a lower press box.

Enter our Fielding Runs Above Average (FRAA). For most positions, FRAA is built from play-by-play data, which allows us to avoid the subjectivity found in many other fielding metrics. The idea is this: count how many fielding plays are made by a given player and compare that to expected plays for an average fielder at their position (based on pitcher ground ball tendencies and batter handedness). Then we adjust for park and base-out situations.

When it comes to catchers, our methodology is a little different thanks to the laundry list of responsibilities they're tasked with beyond just, well, catching and throwing the ball. By now you've probably heard about "framing" or the art of making umpires more likely to call balls outside the strike zone for strikes. To put this into one tidy number, we incorporate pitch tracking data (for the years it exists) and adjust for important factors like pitcher, umpire, batter and home-field advantage using a mixed-model approach. This grants us a number for how many strikes the catcher is personally adding to (or subtracting from) his pitchers' performance … which we then convert to runs added or lost using linear weights.

Framing is one of the biggest parts of determining catcher value, but we also take into account blocking balls from going past, whether a scorer deems it a passed ball or a wild pitch. We use a similar approach—one that really benefits from the pitch tracking data that tells us what ends up in the dirt and what doesn't. We also include a catcher's ability to prevent stolen bases and how well they field balls in play, and *finally* we come up with our FRAA for catchers.

Pitching

Both pitching and fielding make up the half of baseball that isn't run scoring: run prevention. Separating pitching from fielding is a tough task, and most recent pitching analysis has branched off from Voros McCracken's famous (and controversial) statement, "There is little if any difference among major-league pitchers in their ability to prevent hits on balls hit in the field of play." The research of the analytic community has validated this to some extent, and there are a host of "defense-independent" pitching measures that have been developed to try and extract the effect of the defense behind a hurler from the pitcher's work.

Our solution to this quandary is Deserved Run Average (DRA), our core pitching metric. DRA seeks to evaluate a pitcher's performance, much like earned run average (ERA), the tried-and-true pitching stat you've seen on every baseball broadcast or box score from the past century, but it's very different. To start, DRA takes an event-by-event look at what the pitchers does, and adjusts the value of that event based on different environmental factors like park, batter, catcher, umpire, base-out situation, run differential, inning, defense, home field advantage, pitcher role and temperature. That mixed model gives us a pitcher's expected contribution, similar to what we do for our DRC+ model for hitters and FRAA model for catchers. (Oh, and we also consider the pitcher's effect on basestealing and on balls getting past the catcher.)

DRA is set to the scale of runs allowed per nine innings (RA9) instead of ERA, which makes DRA's scale slightly higher than ERA's. Because of this, for ease of use, we're supplying DRA-, which is much easier for the reader to parse. As with DRC+, DRA- is an "index" stat, meaning instead of using some arbitrary and shifting number to denote what's "good," average is always 100. The reason that it uses a minus rather than a plus is because like ERA, a lower number is better. Therefore a 75 DRA- describes a performance 25 percent better than average, whereas a 150 DRA- means that either a pitcher is getting extremely lucky with their results, or getting ready to try a new pitch.

Since the last time you picked up an edition of this book, we've also made a few minor changes to DRA to make it better. Recent research into "tunneling"—the act of throwing consecutive pitches that appear similar from a batter's point of view until after the swing decision point–data has given us a new contextual factor to account for in DRA: plate distance. This refers to the distance between successive pitches as they approach the plate, and while it has a smaller effect than factors like velocity or whiff rate, it still can help explain pitcher strikeout rate in our model.

Recently Added Descriptive Statistics

Returning to our 2021 edition of the book are a few figures which recently appeared. These numbers may be a little bit more familiar to those of you who have spent some time investigating baseball statistics.

Fastball Percentage

Our fastball percentage (FA%) statistic measures how frequently a pitcher throws a pitch classified as a "fastball," measured as a percentage of overall pitches thrown. We qualify three types of fastballs:

1. The traditional four-seam fastball;
2. The two-seam fastball or sinker;
3. "Hard cutters," which are pitches that have the movement profile of a cut fastball and are used as the pitcher's primary offering or in place of a more traditional fastball.

For example, a pitcher with a FA% of 67 throws any combination of these three pitches about two-thirds of the time.

Whiff Rate

Everybody loves a swing and a miss, and whiff rate (Whiff%) measures how frequently pitchers induce a swinging strike. To calculate Whiff%, we add up all the pitches thrown that ended with a swinging strike, then divide that number by a pitcher's total pitches thrown. Most often, high whiff rates correlate with high strikeout rates (and overall effective pitcher performance).

Called Strike Probability

Called Strike Probability (CSP) is a number that represents the likelihood that all of a pitcher's pitches will be called a strike while controlling for location, pitcher and batter handedness, umpire and count. Here's how it works: on each pitch, our model determines how many times (out of 100) that a similar pitch was called for a strike given those factors mentioned above, and when normalized for each batter's strike zone. Then we average the CSP for all pitches thrown by a pitcher in a season, and that gives us the yearly CSP percentage you see in the stats boxes.

As you might imagine, pitchers with a higher CSP are more likely to work in the zone, where pitchers with a lower CSP are likely locating their pitches outside the normal strike zone, for better or for worse.

Projections

Many of you aren't turning to this book just for a look at what a player has done, but for a look at what a player is going to do: the PECOTA projections. PECOTA, initially developed by Nate Silver (who has moved on to greater fame as a political analyst), consists of three parts:

1. Major-league equivalencies, which use minor-league statistics to project how a player will perform in the major leagues;
2. Baseline forecasts, which use weighted averages and regression to the mean to estimate a player's current true talent level; and
3. Aging curves, which uses the career paths of comparable players to estimate how a player's statistics are likely to change over time.

With all those important things covered, let's take a look at what's in the book this year.

Team Prospectus

Most of this book is composed of team chapters, with one for each of the 30 major-league franchises. On the first page of each chapter, you'll see a box that contains some of the key statistics for each team as well as a very inviting stadium diagram.

We start with the team name, their unadjusted 2020 win-loss record, and their divisional ranking. Beneath that are a host of other team statistics. **Pythag** presents an adjusted 2020 winning percentage, calculated by taking runs scored per game (**RS/G**) and runs allowed per game (**RA/G**) for the team, and running them through a version of Bill James' Pythagorean formula that was refined and improved by David Smyth and Brandon Heipp. (The formula is called "Pythagenpat," which is equally fun to type and to say.)

Next up is **DRC+**, described earlier, to indicate the overall hitting ability of the team either above or below league-average. Run prevention on the pitching side is covered by **DRA** (also mentioned earlier) and another metric: Fielding Independent Pitching (**FIP**), which calculates another ERA-like statistic based on strikeouts, walks, and home runs recorded. Defensive Efficiency Rating (**DER**) tells us the percentage of balls in play turned into outs for the team, and is a quick fielding shorthand that rounds out run prevention.

After that, we have several measures related to roster composition, as opposed to on-field performance. **B-Age** and **P-Age** tell us the average age of a team's batters and pitchers, respectively. **Payroll** is the combined team payroll for all on-field players, and Doug Pappas' Marginal Dollars per Marginal Win (**M$/MW**) tells us how much money a team spent to earn production above replacement level.

Next to each of these stats, we've listed each team's MLB rank in that category from first to 30th. In this, first always indicates a positive outcome and 30th a negative outcome, except in the case of salary—first is highest.

After the franchise statistics, we share a few items about the team's home ballpark. There's the aforementioned diagram of the park's dimensions (including distances to the outfield wall), a graphic showing the height of the wall from the left-field pole to the right-field pole, and a table showing three-year park factors for the stadium. The park factors are displayed as indexes where 100 is average, 110 means that the park inflates the statistic in question by 10 percent, and 90 means that the park deflates the statistic in question by 10 percent.

On the second page of each team chapter, you'll find three graphs. The first is **Payroll History** and helps you see how the team's payroll has compared to the MLB and divisional average payrolls over time. Payroll figures are current as of January 1, 2021; with so many free agents still unsigned as of this writing, the final 2021 figure will likely be significantly different for many teams. (In the meantime, you can always find the most current data at Baseball Prospectus' Cot's Baseball Contracts page.)

The second graph is **Future Commitments** and helps you see the team's future outlays, if any.

The third graph is **Farm System Ranking** and displays how the Baseball Prospectus prospect team has ranked the organization's farm system since 2007.

After the graphs, we have a **Personnel** section that lists many of the important decision-makers and upper-level field and operations staff members for the franchise, as well as any former Baseball Prospectus staff members who are currently part of the organization. (In very rare circumstances, someone might be on both lists!)

Position Players

After all that information and a thoughtful bylined essay covering each team, we present our player comments. These are also bylined, but due to frequent franchise shifts during the offseason, our bylines are more a rough guide than a perfect accounting of who wrote what.

Each player is listed with the major-league team that employed him as of early January 2021. If a player changed teams after that point via free agency, trade, or any other method, you'll be able to find them in the chapter for their previous squad.

As an example, take a look at the player comment for Padres shortstop Fernando Tatis Jr.: the stat block that accompanies his written comment is at the top of this page. First we cover biographical information (age is as of June 30, 2021) before moving onto the stats themselves. Our statistic columns include standard identifying information like **YEAR**, **TEAM**, **LVL** (level of affiliated play) and **AGE** before getting into the numbers. Next, we provide raw, untranslated

Fernando Tatis Jr. SS

Born: 01/02/99   Age: 22   Bats: R   Throws: R
Height: 6'3"   Weight: 217   Origin: International Free Agent, 2015

YEAR	TEAM	LVL	AGE	PA	R	2B	3B	HR	RBI	BB	K	SB	CS	AVG/OBP/SLG
2018	SA	AA	19	394	77	22	4	16	43	33	109	16	5	.286/.355/.507
2019	SD	MLB	20	372	61	13	6	22	53	30	110	16	6	.317/.379/.590
2020	SD	MLB	21	257	50	11	2	17	45	27	61	11	3	.277/.366/.571
2021 FS	SD	MLB	22	600	95	24	4	31	81	50	165	17	8	.263/.331/.499
2021 DC	SD	MLB	22	628	100	25	4	32	85	53	173	19	8	.263/.331/.499

Comparables: Darryl Strawberry, Bo Bichette, Ronald Acuña Jr.

YEAR	TEAM	LVL	AGE	PA	DRC+	BABIP	BRR	FRAA	WARP
2018	SA	AA	19	394	136	.370	3.0	SS(83): -1.9	2.4
2019	SD	MLB	20	372	118	.410	7.1	SS(83): 0.9	3.4
2020	SD	MLB	21	257	126	.306	0.7	SS(57): -5.5	0.9
2021 FS	SD	MLB	22	600	126	.318	1.7	SS -1	3.9
2021 DC	SD	MLB	22	628	126	.318	1.8	SS -1	4.0

numbers like you might find on the back of your dad's baseball cards: **PA** (plate appearances), **R** (runs), **2B** (doubles), **3B** (triples), **HR** (home runs), **RBI** (runs batted in), **BB** (walks), **K** (strikeouts), **SB** (stolen bases) and **CS** (caught stealing).

Following the basic stats is **Whiff%** (whiff rate), which denotes how often, when a batter swings, he fails to make contact with the ball. Another way to think of this number is an inverse of a hitter's contact rate.

Next, we have unadjusted "slash" statistics: **AVG** (batting average), **OBP** (on-base percentage) and **SLG** (slugging percentage). Following the slash line is **DRC+** (Deserved Runs Created Plus), which we described earlier as total offensive expected contribution compared to the league average.

BABIP (batting average on balls in play) tells us how often a ball in play fell for a hit, and can help us identify whether a batter may have been lucky or not ... but note that high BABIPs also tend to follow the great hitters of our time, as well as speedy singles hitters who put the ball on the ground.

The next item is **BRR** (Baserunning Runs), which covers all of a player's baserunning accomplishments including (but not limited to) swiped bags and failed attempts. Next is **FRAA** (Fielding Runs Above Average), which also includes the number of games previously played at each position noted in parentheses. Multi-position players have only their two most frequent positions listed here, but their total FRAA number reflects all positions played.

Our last column here is **WARP** (Wins Above Replacement Player). WARP estimates the total value of a player, which means for hitters it takes into account hitting runs above average (calculated using the DRC+ model), BRR and FRAA. Then, it makes an adjustment for positions played and gives the player a credit for plate appearances based upon the difference between "replacement level"—which is derived from the quality of players added to a team's roster after the start of the season–and the league average.

The final line just below the stats box is **PECOTA** data, which is discussed further in a following section.

Catchers

Catchers are a special breed, and thus they have earned their own separate box which displays some of the defensive metrics that we've built just for them. As an example, let's check out Yasmani Grandal.

YEAR	TEAM	P. COUNT	FRM RUNS	BLK RUNS	THRW RUNS	TOT RUNS
2018	LAD	16816	15.7	0.8	0.1	16.5
2019	MIL	18740	19.4	1.8	-0.1	21.1
2020	CHW	4830	3.7	0.3	-0.2	3.8
2021	CHW	14430	16.7	-0.6	1.0	17.1
2021	CHW	14430	16.7	0.4	1.0	18.0

The **YEAR** and **TEAM** columns match what you'd find in the other stat box. **P. COUNT** indicates the number of pitches thrown while the catcher was behind the plate, including swinging strikes, fouls and balls in play. **FRM RUNS** is the total run value the catcher provided (or cost) his team by influencing the umpire to call strikes where other catchers did not. **BLK RUNS** expresses the total run value above or below average for the catcher's ability to prevent wild pitches and passed balls. **THRW RUNS** is calculated using a similar model as the previous two statistics, and it measures a catcher's ability to throw out basestealers but also to dissuade them from testing his arm in the first place. It takes into account factors like the pitcher (including his delivery and pickoff move) and baserunner (who could be as fast as Billy Hamilton or as slow as Yonder Alonso). **TOT RUNS** is the sum of all of the previous three statistics.

Pitchers

Let's give our pitchers a turn, using 2020 AL Cy Young winner Shane Bieber as our example. Take a look at his stat block: the first line and the **YEAR**, **TEAM**, **LVL** and **AGE** columns are the same as in the position player example earlier.

Here too, we have a series of columns that display raw, unadjusted statistics compiled by the pitcher over the course of a season: **W** (wins), **L** (losses), **SV** (saves), **G** (games pitched), **GS** (games started), **IP** (innings pitched), **H** (hits allowed) and **HR** (home runs allowed). Next we have two statistics that are rates: **BB/9** (walks per nine innings) and **K/9** (strikeouts per nine innings), before returning to the unadjusted K (strikeouts).

Next up is **GB%** (ground ball percentage), which is the percentage of all batted balls that were hit on the ground, including both outs and hits. Remember, this is based on observational data and subject to human error, so please approach this with a healthy dose of skepticism.

BABIP (batting average on balls in play) is calculated using the same methodology as it is for position players, but it often tells us more about a pitcher than it does a hitter. With pitchers, a high BABIP is often due to poor defense or bad luck, and can often be an indicator of potential rebound, and a low BABIP may be cause to expect performance regression. (A typical league-average BABIP is close to .290-.300.)

The metrics **WHIP** (walks plus hits per inning pitched) and **ERA** (earned run average) are old standbys: WHIP measures walks and hits allowed on a per-inning basis, while ERA measures earned runs on a nine-inning basis. Neither of these stats are translated or adjusted.

DRA- (Deserved Run Average) was described at length earlier, and measures how the pitcher "deserved" to perform compared to other pitchers. Please note that since we lack all the data points that would make for a "real" DRA for minor-league events, the DRA- displayed for minor league partial-seasons is based off of different data. (That data is a modified version of our cFIP metric, which you can find more information about on our website.)

Shane Bieber   RHP

Born: 05/31/95   Age: 26   Bats: R   Throws: R
Height: 6'3"   Weight: 200   Origin: Round 4, 2016 Draft (#122 overall)

YEAR	TEAM	LVL	AGE	W	L	SV	G	GS	IP	H	HR	BB/9	K/9	K	GB%	BABIP
2018	AKR	AA	23	3	0	0	5	5	31	26	1	0.3	8.7	30	47.3%	.278
2018	COL	AAA	23	3	1	0	8	8	48[2]	30	3	1.1	8.7	47	52.0%	.227
2018	CLE	MLB	23	11	5	0	20	19	114[2]	130	13	1.8	9.3	118	46.2%	.356
2019	CLE	MLB	24	15	8	0	34	33	214[1]	186	31	1.7	10.9	259	44.4%	.298
2020	CLE	MLB	25	8	1	0	12	12	77[1]	46	7	2.4	14.2	122	48.4%	.267
2021 FS	CLE	MLB	26	10	6	0	26	26	150	121	18	2.1	11.7	195	45.5%	.297
2021 DC	CLE	MLB	26	14	7	0	30	30	196.7	159	24	2.1	11.7	257	45.5%	.297

Comparables: Luis Severino, Danny Salazar, Joe Musgrove

YEAR	TEAM	LVL	AGE	WHIP	ERA	DRA-	WARP	MPH	FB%	WHF	CSP
2018	AKR	AA	23	0.87	1.16	61	0.9				
2018	COL	AAA	23	0.74	1.66	69	1.2				
2018	CLE	MLB	23	1.33	4.55	74	2.6	94.7	57.4%	26.2%	
2019	CLE	MLB	24	1.05	3.28	75	4.9	94.4	45.8%	30.8%	
2020	CLE	MLB	25	0.87	1.63	53	2.6	95.3	53.6%	40.7%	
2021 FS	CLE	MLB	26	1.04	2.44	64	4.4	94.7	50.0%	33.2%	44.2%
2021 DC	CLE	MLB	26	1.04	2.44	64	5.8	94.7	50.0%	33.2%	44.2%

Just like with hitters, **WARP** (Wins Above Replacement Player) is a total value metric that puts pitchers of all stripes on the same scale as position players. We use DRA as the primary input for our calculation of WARP. You might notice that relief pitchers (due to their limited innings) may have a lower WARP than you were expecting or than you might see in other WARP-like metrics. WARP does not take leverage into account, just the actions a pitcher performs and the expected value of those actions ... which ends up judging high-leverage relief pitchers differently than you might imagine given their prestige and market value.

MPH gives you the pitcher's 95th percentile velocity for the noted season, in order to give you an idea of what the *peak* fastball velocity a pitcher possesses. Since this comes from our pitch-tracking data, it is not publicly available for minor-league pitchers.

Finally, we display the three new pitching metrics we described earlier. **FB%** (fastball percentage) gives you the percentage of fastballs thrown out of all pitches. **WHF** (whiff rate) tells you the percentage of swinging strikes induced out of all pitches. **CSP** (called strike probability) expresses the likelihood of all pitches thrown to result in a called strike, after controlling for factors like handedness, umpire, pitch type, count and location.

PECOTA

All players have PECOTA projections for 2021, as well as a set of other numbers that describe the performance of comparable players according to PECOTA. All projections for 2021 are for the player at the date we went to press in early January and are projected into the league and park context as indicated by the team abbreviation. (Note that players at very low levels of the minors are too unpredictable to assess using these numbers.) All PECOTA projected statistics represent a player's projected major-league performance.

How we're doing that is a little different this season. There are really two different values that go into the final stat line that you see for PECOTA: How a player performs, and how much playing time he'll be given to perform it. In the past we've estimated playing time based on each team's roster and depth charts, and we'll continue to do that. These projections are denoted as **2021 DC**.

But in many cases, a player won't be projected for major-league playing time; most of the time this is because they aren't projected to be major-league players at all, but still developing as prospects. Or perhaps a player will provide Triple-A depth, only to have an opportunity open up because of injury. For these purposes, we're also supplying a second projection, labeled **2021 FS**, or full season. This is what we would project the player to provide in 600 plate appearances or 150 innings pitched.

Below the projections are the player's three highest-scoring comparable players as determined by PECOTA. All comparables represent a snapshot of how the listed player was performing at the same age as the current player, so if a

23-year-old pitcher is compared to Bartolo Colón, he's actually being compared to a 23-year-old Colón, not the version that pitched for the Rangers in 2018, nor to Colón's career as a whole.

A few points about pitcher projections. First, we aren't yet projecting peak velocity, so that column will be blank in the PECOTA lines. Second, projecting DRA is trickier than evaluating past performance, because it is unclear how deserving each pitcher will be of his anticipated outcomes. However, we know that another DRA-related statistic–contextual FIP or cFIP-estimates future run scoring very well. So for PECOTA, the projected DRA- figures you see are based on the past cFIPs generated by the pitcher and comparable players over time, along with the other factors described above.

If you're familiar with PECOTA, then you'll have noticed that the projection system often appears bullish on players coming off a bad year and bearish on players coming off a good year. (This is because the system weights several previous seasons, not just the most recent one.) In addition, we publish the 50th percentile projections for each player–which is smack in the middle of the range of projected production—which tends to mean PECOTA stat lines don't often have extreme results like 40 home runs or 250 strikeouts in a given season. In essence, PECOTA doesn't project very many extreme seasons.

Managers

After all those wonderful team chapters, we've got statistics for each big-league manager, all of whom are organized by alphabetical order. Here you'll find a block including an extraordinary amount of information collected from each manager's entire career. For more information on the acronyms and what they mean, please visit the Glossary at www.baseballprospectus.com.

There is one important metric that we'd like to call attention to, and you'll find it next to each manager's name: **wRM+** (weighted reliever management plus). Developed by Rob Arthur and Rian Watt, wRM+ investigates how good a manager is at using their best relievers during the moments of highest leverage, using both our proprietary DRA metric as well as Leverage Index. wRM+ is scaled to a league average of 100, and a wRM+ of 105 indicates that relievers were used approximately five percent "better" than average. On the other hand, a wRM+ of 95 would tell us the team used its relievers five percent "worse" than the average team.

While wRM+ does not have an extremely strong correlation with a manager, it is statistically significant; this means that a manager is not *entirely* responsible for a team's wRM+, but does have some effect on that number.

Part 1: Team Analysis

Performance Graphs

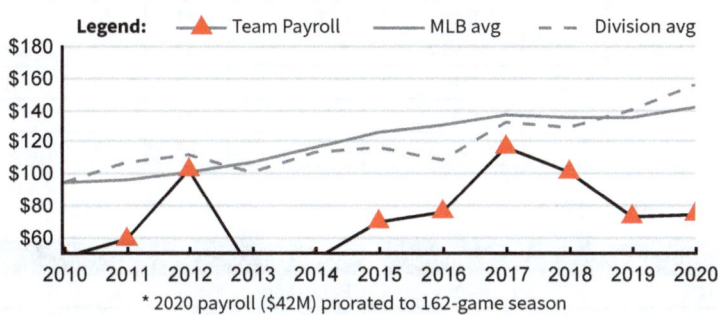

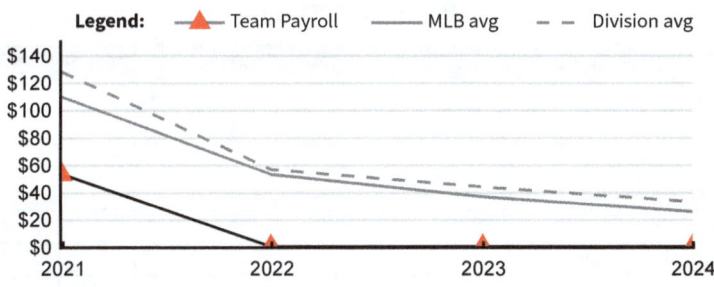

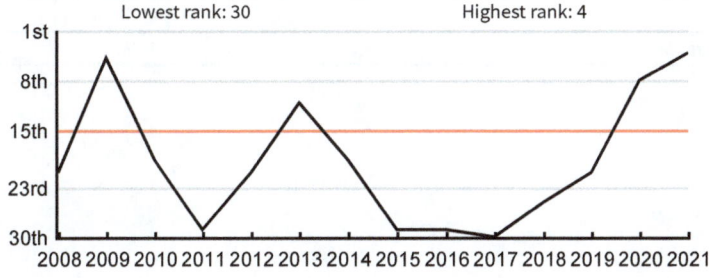

2020 Team Performance

ACTUAL STANDINGS

Team	W	L	Pct
ATL	35	25	0.583
MIA	**31**	**29**	**0.517**
PHI	28	32	0.467
NYM	26	34	0.433
WAS	26	34	0.433

dWIN% STANDINGS

Team	W	L	Pct
PHI	34	26	0.580
ATL	33	27	0.562
NYM	32	28	0.549
WAS	27	33	0.450
MIA	**25**	**35**	**0.431**

TOP HITTERS

Player	WARP
Miguel Rojas	1.5
Brian Anderson	1.4
Jesús Aguilar	0.5

TOP PITCHERS

Player	WARP
Pablo López	1.4
Sixto Sánchez	0.8
Sandy Alcantara	0.7

VITAL STATISTICS

Statistic Name	Value	Rank
Pythagenpat	.431	24th
dWin%	.431	20th
Runs Scored per Game	4.38	21st
Runs Allowed per Game	5.07	22nd
Deserved Runs Created Plus	94	22nd
Deserved Run Average Minus	101	17th
Fielding Independent Pitching	5.00	25th
Defensive Efficiency Rating	.688	25th
Batter Age	29.4	20th
Pitcher Age	27.4	2nd
Payroll	$42.0M	23rd
Marginal $ per Marginal Win	$1.9M	6th

2021 Team Projections

PROJECTED STANDINGS

Team	W	L	Pct	+/-
NYM	93.6	68.4	0.578	23
Their additions should yield the best Mets team since 2015, even if their competition in the NL East is much stiffer than it was then.				
WAS	84.7	77.3	0.523	14
Mike Rizzo remade the middle of his lineup and improved the pitching staff, but given the caliber of their competition he could have aimed a hair higher.				
PHI	83.8	78.2	0.517	8
Re-signing J.T. Realmuto and Didi Gregorius keeps the offense intact, but has Dave Dombrowski successfully built a bullpen?				
ATL	81.5	80.5	0.503	-13
The rotation and positional stars set a high floor; their role players will determine their ceiling.				
MIA	70.9	91.1	0.438	-12
Hired a transformational leader and then did nothing to improve (or even reshape) a middling roster.				

TOP PROJECTED HITTERS

Player	WARP
Starling Marte	3.3
Brian Anderson	2.1
Adam Duvall	1.9

TOP PROJECTED PITCHERS

Player	WARP
Sixto Sánchez	2.1
Pablo López	2.0
Elieser Hernandez	1.9

FARM SYSTEM REPORT

Top Prospect	Number of Top 101 Prospects
Sixto Sánchez, #4	6

KEY DEDUCTIONS

Player	WARP
José Ureña	0.5
Ryne Stanek	0.4

KEY ADDITIONS

Player	WARP
Anthony Bass	0.8
Dylan Floro	0.7
Adam Cimber	0.6

Team Personnel

Chief Executive Officer
Derek Jeter

General Manager
Kim Ng

Assistant General Manager
Daniel Greenlee

Assistant General Manager
Brian Chattin

Vice President, Player Development and Scouting
Gary Denbo

Manager
Don Mattingly

BP Alumni
John Eshleman

Marlins Park Stats

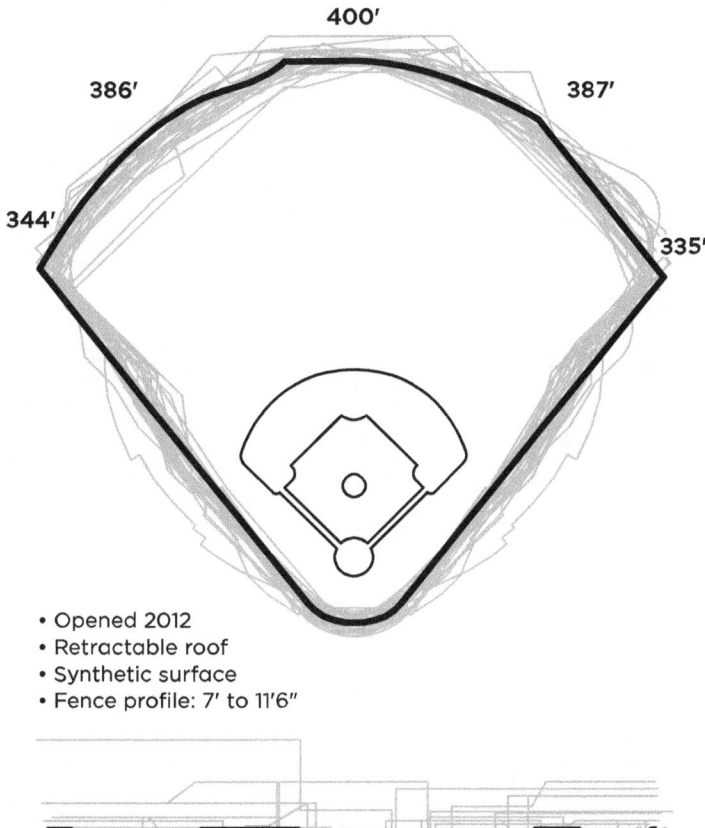

- Opened 2012
- Retractable roof
- Synthetic surface
- Fence profile: 7' to 11'6"

Three-Year Park Factors

Runs	Runs/RH	Runs/LH	HR/RH	HR/LH
95	95	94	87	91

Marlins Team Analysis

The 2020 baseball season was built to erase its own context.

It all looked ridiculous, of course, through a lens that looked either backward or forward: *What would you think if you saw this last year?* ("Ah, yeah, this is just the 60-game scramble-season we're playing amid a global pandemic.") How would you read this in the history books? ("After months on pause, some entertainment industries resumed with modifications, such as baseball stadiums filled with cardboard cutouts instead of fans.") But watching through the lens of someone who was there in real time, against the backdrop of real life, it looked … like baseball. If you wanted, or needed, to forget everything else, you could. The broadcast was aimed squarely on the field with little reference to the stuffed animals in the seats. The video-game soundtrack seemed normal after a brief period of adjustment. The new rules and abbreviated doubleheaders could be discussed as on-the-field matters with minimal reference to why they were necessary. And so it went—an elbow bump doesn't look so different from a handshake, and a neck gaiter isn't weird in Ohio in April, so really, how much magical thinking does it take to get used to it in Texas in July? It was baseball. All the rest was only as noticeable as you wanted it to be.

That the season can be viewed as just baseball is obvious in the fact that any version of this book can exist at all. But the ability to view it this way falls apart when it comes to the Marlins. From start to finish, their season was shaped by these external forces, providing their central conflict, the scrambled outline of their schedule, the emotional thrust for their eventual playoff berth. The Marlins were the first North American major professional sports team to experience an in-season outbreak of the coronavirus and therefore also the first to see the other side of that. There can be no honest attempt to view any of this as strictly baseball. So how are you supposed to remember the 2020 Miami Marlins?

⚾ ⚾ ⚾

The place to begin is probably the hotel. (As it happens, the hotel is also the place where it almost ended, but that is neither here nor there.) In late July and early August, the Marlins spent more than a week at the Rittenhouse Hotel in Philadelphia, isolated both from baseball and from the rest of the world with an outbreak of COVID-19.

Miami Marlins 2021

The Marlins had arrived at the hotel before their Opening Day game against the Phillies on July 24. By July 26, four players learned that they had tested positive for the coronavirus, including scheduled starter José Ureña. The team made a few substitutions and played anyway. By July 27, the number of positive tests in their traveling party had hit 13, which would soon be 17, which would soon be 21. The Marlins stopped playing. Instead, they stayed in the hotel, left to wait without much sense of just what they were waiting for.

They were waiting as sickness requires anyone to wait—waiting to learn just who had been infected and hoping for health to be restored. But they were also waiting to be able to play baseball again, and on this point, there was no clarity. While MLB's detailed handbook of coronavirus protocol offered how to flush an airplane toilet (be sure to shut it first), and how to label the hand sanitizer in the dugout ("conspicuous signage"), it did not share anything specific on how to navigate an outbreak. There was no threshold at which a team's season would be cancelled and no timeline for when its season could restart. If half your roster was out—and, for the Marlins, *more* than half the roster was—you'd simply have to build a new one. If your schedule was wrecked, you'd build a new one of those, too. Or maybe you wouldn't. Maybe it would all go the other way—no roster, no schedule, no season. Who could tell? There was no specific marker to count down to or count up for and no idea of which way to look.

Instead, there was the hotel. There was the wait.

There has been some academic debate on the subject of whether hotels qualify as liminal spaces. A liminal space is designed for transition; it's a hallway, a waiting room, a highway rest stop. These are places that you are meant to pass through rather than stay inside. A hotel *can* fit this definition—your stay is meant to be temporary—but the fit is not ideal. A hotel is not so explicitly transitory as those other locations: it's part of the destination rather than the journey, and sometimes, it *is* the destination. A hotel may not have a particularly strong sense of place, but it will still feel like *a* place, in a way that a transitional area like a corridor will not.

This makes a hotel a curious space to wait for something. It's a comfortable place to stay, of course, because it has to be. But so much of that comfort is dependent on the knowledge of a checkout time. An indefinite wait on terms that no one knows over a process that cannot be controlled? That's not meant for a hotel.

The French anthropologist Marc Augé suggested a different category of space for a hotel—not a liminal space but a "non-place." His distinction is a very academic one (Augé introduced the idea in a 1995 essay titled "Non-Places: An Introduction to Supermodernity") but the core of it feels relevant here:

> "The space of non-place creates neither singular identity nor relations; only solitude, and similitude. There is no room for history unless it has been transformed into an element of spectacle, usually in allusive texts. What reigns there is actuality, the urgency of the present moment. Since non-places are there to be passed through, they are measured in units of time."

This feels closer to the Marlins' stay in the Rittenhouse Hotel: waiting in a non-place, in their non-season, for this non-baseball.

The baseball season has little use for traditional units of time. "An hour" does not mean as much as "three innings"; a few days does not mean as much as a series; a week does not mean as much as a road trip. An off day is not defined by "day" so much as it is by "off." The schedule is its own calendar. In the hotel, however, all this was useless. Here, the Marlins were stuck in "actuality, the urgency of the present moment"—a non-place, just passing through, without a timeline or deadline or lifeline.

"I don't put this in the nightmare category," Commissioner Rob Manfred would tell ESPN in the middle of the hotel stay. "It's not a positive thing, but I don't see it as a nightmare."

The statement justifiably received a little scorn. (One shudders to think of Manfred's dreams if "Miami Marlins indefinitely stranded in makeshift quarantine unit due to viral outbreak" does not qualify as a nightmare.) But the assessment of the situation was more accurate than it might have sounded initially. An extended stay in a liminal space, passing through a non-place, isn't a *nightmare*. There are no horror-film jump cuts or physical frights here. But it does not feel like anything you could find in regular waking life, and if it's dreamlike, it's certainly not enjoyable.

⚾ ⚾ ⚾

The Marlins checked out and left Philadelphia in early August. The team arranged a set of sleeper buses for the infected players to make the 17-hour drive back to Miami; if the question of who would drive these buses seems important, much like the question of who had been asked to work in the hotel that had unexpectedly become a quarantine unit, it was never centered as such. Instead, the center of the situation was now baseball, and all the rest was only as noticeable as you wanted it to be.

If it feels like it would be difficult *not* to notice all the rest under these circumstances—well, again, this was a season built to erase its own context. The Marlins tried to proceed as normally as a team possibly could. They needed a new roster, so they promoted some players from the alternate training site and picked up a few more on waivers and selected the contracts of some others. They needed to play 57 games in 55 days, so they got a new schedule that would allow them to do just that, crammed with abbreviated doubleheaders. Thusly, Miami set out to contend for its first playoff berth in more than a decade, a goal that had been made newly feasible by the news that the postseason would conveniently expand this year.

This was ridiculous. All of it—absurd, an affront to any principle of competitive integrity and to the general idea that a season like this could be pulled off convincingly. If you were trying to maintain the illusion that this was just baseball, cropping out the empty stadiums and papering over the adjusted schedule, that illusion shattered with the Marlins. Their situation could not be ignored. If you were turning to this season in search of normal baseball, and therefore normal life, you instead would see only a joke. (Whether the joke was funny or in poor taste was a matter of interpretation.) You would instead see these Marlins.

They were not quite a *team*, at least not as the term is typically understood, with 61 players needed to make it through 60 games. There was no sense of narrative cohesion around these moves; Miami swapped guys out with abandon, spinning through the injured list, picking up other clubs' flotsam while it waited to retrieve its own jetsam. If you were devoted to trying to view this season logically, you would probably assume that this went rather poorly, given everything known about every variable involved. And, of course, you would be wrong. This was a playoff team! How could it be anything else?

The Marlins' postseason chances had been clocked at next to zero at the start of the season, and after their indefinite break and roster remodel, they played roughly as originally expected, with below-average team performances for both offense and pitching. Their -41 run differential would be the worst of any playoff team in history. So, naturally, despite all this, they won and kept winning. They worked to win even more with the deadline acquisition of Starling Marte. (Another surprise that could not be easily dismissed—"What are the Marlins more likely to do next season, trade for the most desirable hitter available on the market, or charter a special plague bus to drive down the East Coast?" might have been a genuinely difficult question to answer in December 2019.) They made the postseason comfortably, not squeaking in as the eighth seed but instead grabbing the sixth, even advancing to the next round. Here was another illusion shattered—there was no sanctity to these playoffs. The baseball was not normal and neither was it particularly rational.

It was baseball, but *not*, generally taking the right shape but hitting the wrong notes and missing the typical relationships to space and identity and logic. It would have been unthinkable looking forward and might eventually be horrific looking backward, but when you were looking at it head on in actuality, in the urgency of the present moment, it was simply weird. The Marlins had passed through a non-place and ended up playing non-baseball. It was a joke that you were not supposed to get. It wasn't a nightmare, but it wasn't much of anything else, either.

Which is all to say—it was baseball. All the rest was only as noticeable as you wanted it to be.

—Emma Baccellieri is an author at Sports Illustrated.

Part 2: Player Analysis

PLAYER COMMENTS WITH GRAPHS

Jesús Aguilar 1B
Born: 06/30/90   Age: 31   Bats: R   Throws: R
Height: 6'3"   Weight: 277   Origin: International Free Agent, 2007

YEAR	TEAM	LVL	AGE	PA	R	2B	3B	HR	RBI	BB	K	SB	CS	AVG/OBP/SLG
2018	MIL	MLB	28	566	80	25	0	35	108	58	143	0	0	.274/.352/.539
2019	MIL	MLB	29	262	26	9	0	8	34	31	59	0	0	.225/.320/.374
2019	TB	MLB	29	107	13	3	0	4	16	12	22	0	0	.261/.336/.424
2020	MIA	MLB	30	216	31	10	0	8	34	23	40	0	1	.277/.352/.457
2021 FS	MIA	MLB	31	600	77	24	1	26	78	59	143	0	1	.245/.328/.443
2021 DC	MIA	MLB	31	413	53	16	0	17	54	40	98	0	0	.245/.328/.443

Comparables: Tony Clark, Justin Bour, Steve Balboni

Miami plucked Aguilar off waivers last offseason from Tampa Bay's carousel of cheap first basemen, hoping he'd bounce back from a troubled 2019. He didn't quite make it all the way back to his homer-fueled All-Star level of production, but he did hit the ball on the ground less and that pushed his output to the middle of the two poles. That made him a perfectly fine first base option, and the surprise introduction of the designated hitter to the National League gave the Marlins a new place to work his bat in. As a free talent pickup, that's as good as you can ask for.

YEAR	TEAM	LVL	AGE	PA	DRC+	BABIP	BRR	FRAA	WARP
2018	MIL	MLB	28	566	135	.309	-1.1	1B(132): 3.6, 3B(5): 0.0	3.6
2019	MIL	MLB	29	262	93	.264	-1.9	1B(60): 0.1, 3B(2): -0.0	0.1
2019	TB	MLB	29	107	104	.290	-1.7	1B(15): -0.0	0.1
2020	MIA	MLB	30	216	115	.306	-0.6	1B(31): -0.3, 3B(1): -0.0	0.5
2021 FS	MIA	MLB	31	600	110	.288	-0.9	1B 0, 3B 0	1.6
2021 DC	MIA	MLB	31	413	110	.288	-0.6	1B 0	1.2

Jesús Aguilar, continued

Batted Ball Distribution

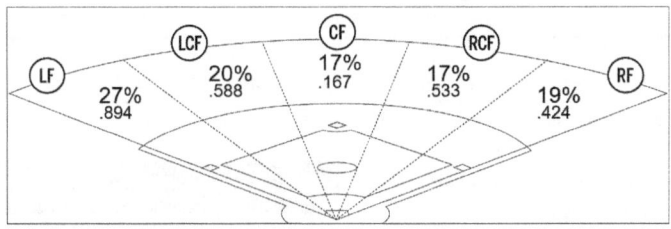

Strike Zone vs LHP   Strike Zone vs RHP

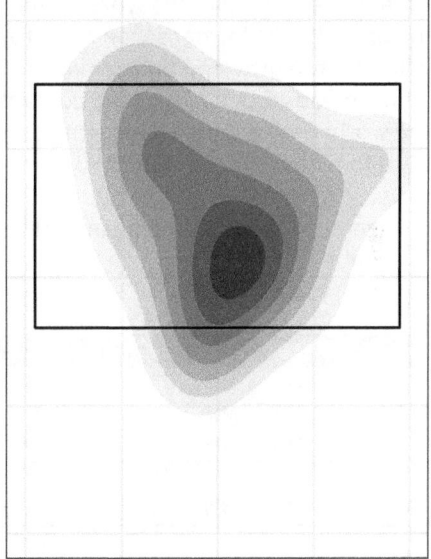

Jorge Alfaro C

Born: 06/11/93 Age: 28 Bats: R Throws: R
Height: 6'3" Weight: 230 Origin: International Free Agent, 2010

YEAR	TEAM	LVL	AGE	PA	R	2B	3B	HR	RBI	BB	K	SB	CS	AVG/OBP/SLG
2018	PHI	MLB	25	377	35	16	2	10	37	18	138	3	0	.262/.324/.407
2019	MIA	MLB	26	465	44	14	1	18	57	22	154	4	4	.262/.312/.425
2020	MIA	MLB	27	100	12	2	0	3	16	4	36	2	0	.226/.280/.344
2021 FS	MIA	MLB	28	600	68	24	2	21	70	29	215	2	1	.238/.297/.404
2021 DC	MIA	MLB	28	408	46	16	1	14	48	20	146	1	1	.238/.297/.404

Comparables: David Ross, John Russell, Mike Zunino

Over the past five seasons, Alfaro has swung at a higher percentage of pitches than any player in baseball and had the third-worst contact rate on them (min. 500 PA). It's a credit to his massive underlying hitting talent that he's only been mediocre in that time frame instead of the worst hitter in baseball. The former seven-time Top 101 prospect strikes out far too much, walks far too little and doesn't lift the ball enough when he does make contact, which means much of his hard contact is on the ground. He hasn't been lighting the world on fire defensively either, despite flashing top-notch framing ability in 2018 to pair with his great agility and arm strength. We've seen enough catchers develop in their late-20s to retain hope that he can all put it together entering his age-28 season but the flashes of supreme upside are starting to look more like embers of what might've been instead of the sparks that will ignite a legendary flame.

YEAR	TEAM	P. COUNT	FRM RUNS	BLK RUNS	THRW RUNS	TOT RUNS
2018	PHI	14249	12.3	-2.4	0.0	9.9
2019	MIA	16970	-1.7	-3.5	0.1	-5.2
2020	MIA	3746	-3.1	0.0	0.0	-3.1
2021	MIA	15632	-0.3	-2.3	0.0	-2.6
2021	MIA	15632	-0.3	-1.9	0.0	-2.1

YEAR	TEAM	LVL	AGE	PA	DRC+	BABIP	BRR	FRAA	WARP
2018	PHI	MLB	25	377	84	.406	0.5	C(104): 12.2, 3B(1): -0.0	2.5
2019	MIA	MLB	26	465	86	.364	-2.1	C(118): -2.0, 1B(1): -0.0	1.1
2020	MIA	MLB	27	100	69	.333	-0.1	C(29): -0.3, RF(1): -0.1	-0.4
2021 FS	MIA	MLB	28	600	91	.350	-0.6	C -2, 1B 0	1.6
2021 DC	MIA	MLB	28	408	91	.350	-0.4	C -2	1.0

Jorge Alfaro, continued

Batted Ball Distribution

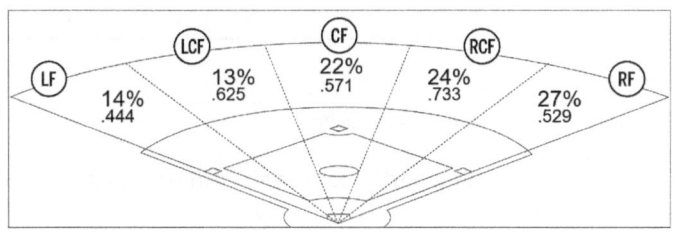

Strike Zone vs LHP   Strike Zone vs RHP

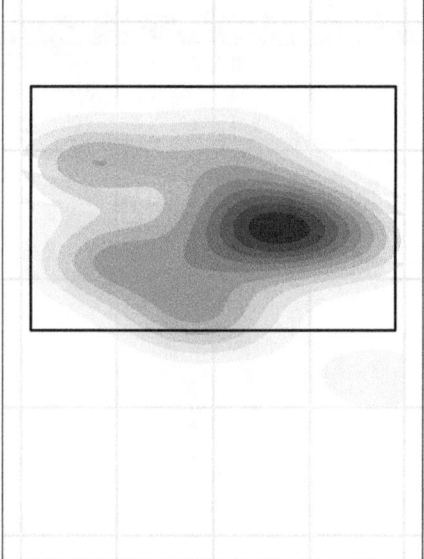

Brian Anderson 3B

Born: 05/19/93   Age: 28   Bats: R   Throws: R
Height: 6'3"   Weight: 208   Origin: Round 3, 2014 Draft (#76 overall)

YEAR	TEAM	LVL	AGE	PA	R	2B	3B	HR	RBI	BB	K	SB	CS	AVG/OBP/SLG
2018	MIA	MLB	25	670	87	34	4	11	65	62	129	2	4	.273/.357/.400
2019	MIA	MLB	26	520	57	33	1	20	66	44	114	5	1	.261/.342/.468
2020	MIA	MLB	27	229	27	7	1	11	38	22	66	0	0	.255/.345/.465
2021 FS	MIA	MLB	28	600	77	27	2	22	78	56	162	2	1	.250/.338/.440
2021 DC	MIA	MLB	28	580	75	26	2	21	76	54	157	2	1	.250/.338/.440

Comparables: Fernando Tatis, Corey Koskie, Howard Johnson

Anderson doesn't do anything particularly well with the stick yet but does absolutely everything well enough, leading to solidly above-average offensive performance every year. His ability to play the outfield when called upon has been masking his stellar infield glove for a few years, and left alone at the hot corner, he snagged a 2020 Gold Glove nomination and led the majors in third base FRAA. He's a very good baseball player without the flash, panache or high-profile posting needed to be a star.

YEAR	TEAM	LVL	AGE	PA	DRC+	BABIP	BRR	FRAA	WARP
2018	MIA	MLB	25	670	108	.332	2.3	RF(91): -1.1, 3B(71): -9.0	1.8
2019	MIA	MLB	26	520	107	.305	2.0	3B(67): 1.1, RF(55): 6.3	3.1
2020	MIA	MLB	27	229	106	.323	0.8	3B(56): 7.5, 1B(1): -0.1, 2B(1): -0.0	1.4
2021 FS	MIA	MLB	28	600	114	.320	-0.6	3B 0, 1B 0	2.2
2021 DC	MIA	MLB	28	580	114	.320	-0.6	3B 0	2.1

Brian Anderson, continued

Batted Ball Distribution

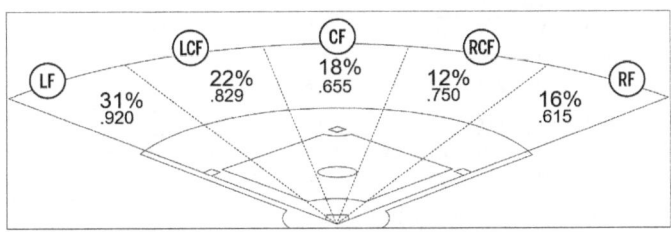

Strike Zone vs LHP   **Strike Zone vs RHP**

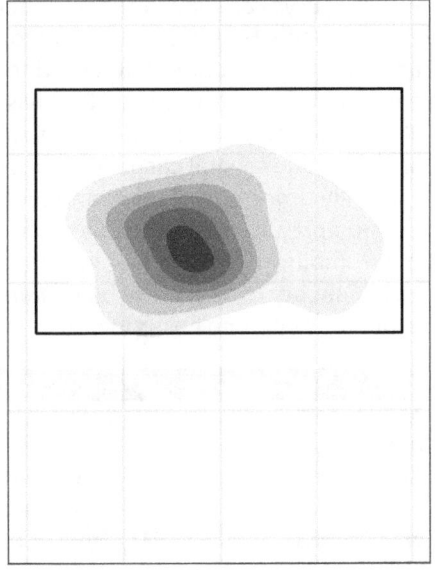

Jon Berti 2B

Born: 01/22/90 Age: 31 Bats: R Throws: R
Height: 5'10" Weight: 190 Origin: Round 18, 2011 Draft (#559 overall)

YEAR	TEAM	LVL	AGE	PA	R	2B	3B	HR	RBI	BB	K	SB	CS	AVG/OBP/SLG
2018	NH	AA	28	316	55	13	7	8	42	29	46	21	9	.314/.399/.498
2018	COL	AAA	28	73	10	1	0	0	3	9	13	8	1	.217/.333/.233
2018	TOR	MLB	28	15	2	1	1	0	2	0	4	1	0	.267/.267/.467
2019	NO	AAA	29	79	14	1	0	4	8	15	11	5	0	.290/.430/.500
2019	MIA	MLB	29	287	52	14	1	6	24	24	73	17	3	.273/.348/.406
2020	MIA	MLB	30	149	21	5	0	2	14	23	37	9	2	.258/.388/.350
2021 FS	MIA	MLB	31	600	75	24	4	12	53	60	155	33	8	.237/.330/.371
2021 DC	MIA	MLB	31	556	70	22	3	11	49	56	143	31	7	.237/.330/.371

Comparables: Jose Valentin, Dale Sveum, Ian Desmond

Just a few minutes before August 25th turned to August 26th, Berti began a great adventure. The Marlins were deep into their second doubleheader in four days, holding a 2-0 lead against the Mets in the sixth inning of the second game, a "home" game played at Citi Field. Berti walked on five pitches against Mets reliever Jeurys Familia, and that's when the Yakety Sax music started. On the very next pitch, Berti scampered off for second and the ball clanked off Ali Sánchez's glove. A batter later, Berti took off for third; the throw would've beaten him if third baseman J.D. Davis had been anywhere near the bag, but he failed to cover in time and Berti was safe again. With Berti now 90 feet away, Sánchez made several casual lobs back to Familia on the mound, and Berti eventually timed one of them and took off on a delayed steal of home. It was a heads-up play, except for the part where Berti tripped halfway down the line. Now stumbling home, he would've been easily out at the plate but for the part where Sánchez dropped the ball *again*. Berti became the first player in franchise history to steal three bases in one inning. And then the clock struck midnight.

YEAR	TEAM	LVL	AGE	PA	DRC+	BABIP	BRR	FRAA	WARP
2018	NH	AA	28	316	152	.354	0.6	3B(27): -0.8, 2B(20): -0.1, CF(7): 0.9	2.2
2018	COL	AAA	28	73	77	.271	-0.5	LF(11): -1.5, 2B(6): -0.2, 3B(4): -0.7	-0.4
2018	TOR	MLB	28	15	85	.364	0.6	2B(4): -0.6	0.0
2019	NO	AAA	29	79	132	.292	1.2	3B(9): -0.4, CF(6): 1.2, SS(5): 0.6	0.8
2019	MIA	MLB	29	287	87	.360	5.0	SS(32): -1.4, CF(21): -1.2, 3B(20): 1.5	1.1
2020	MIA	MLB	30	149	87	.354	0.5	2B(21): -0.4, CF(9): -1.6, RF(7): -0.6	0.2
2021 FS	MIA	MLB	31	600	96	.314	2.6	2B -1, RF -1	1.4
2021 DC	MIA	MLB	31	556	96	.314	2.4	2B -1, RF -1	1.2

Jon Berti, continued

Batted Ball Distribution

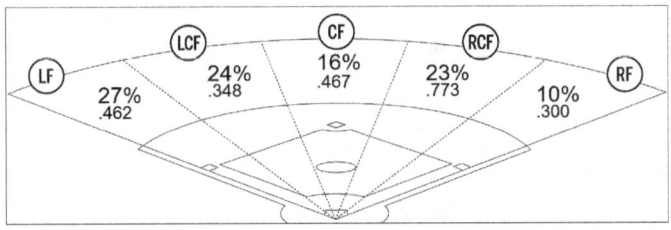

Strike Zone vs LHP   Strike Zone vs RHP

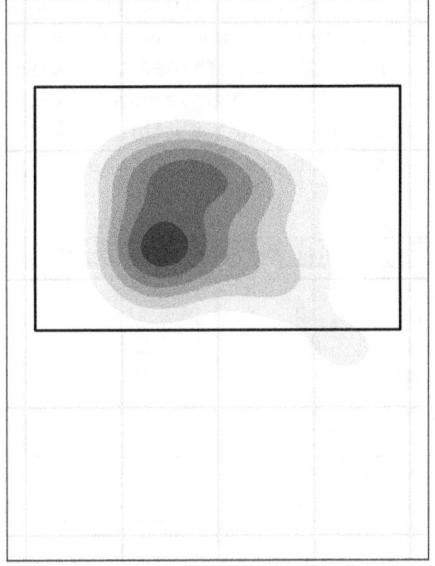

Lewis Brinson CF

Born: 05/08/94   Age: 27   Bats: R   Throws: R
Height: 6'5"   Weight: 212   Origin: Round 1, 2012 Draft (#29 overall)

YEAR	TEAM	LVL	AGE	PA	R	2B	3B	HR	RBI	BB	K	SB	CS	AVG/OBP/SLG
2018	JAX	AA	24	26	1	0	0	1	1	3	5	1	0	.130/.231/.261
2018	NO	AAA	24	27	0	1	1	0	3	0	6	0	0	.222/.222/.333
2018	MIA	MLB	24	406	31	10	5	11	42	17	120	2	1	.199/.240/.338
2019	NO	AAA	25	339	56	15	4	16	56	32	100	16	5	.270/.361/.510
2019	MIA	MLB	25	248	15	9	1	0	15	13	73	1	1	.173/.236/.221
2020	MIA	MLB	26	112	14	6	0	3	12	6	30	4	0	.226/.268/.368
2021 FS	MIA	MLB	27	600	61	26	4	16	64	40	174	6	3	.221/.283/.374
2021 DC	MIA	MLB	27	159	16	6	1	4	16	10	46	1	1	.221/.283/.374

Comparables: Todd Dunwoody, Jason Romano, Ron LeFlore

It's hard for some people to move on from the glories of their past. Imagine how hard it must be to move on from the glories of one's past's future, coming to terms with what you haven't become. Brinson was a top-30 prospect three times as a member of three different organizations (Rangers, Brewers, Marlins). As a prospect, Brinson had a habit of flatlining upon promotion before electroshocking back to life after an adjustment period, but his bat has been fairly unresponsive to medical intervention as a big-leaguer. As it stands, Brinson's legs and glove should keep him on the fringes of the majors as long as he's cheap, and he's not threatening to get expensive with the way he's swinging. His best hope for changing what lies ahead might be to accept what doesn't.

YEAR	TEAM	LVL	AGE	PA	DRC+	BABIP	BRR	FRAA	WARP
2018	JAX	AA	24	26	59	.118	-0.1	CF(8): -1.0	-0.2
2018	NO	AAA	24	27	61	.286	0.0	CF(5): -1.6	-0.2
2018	MIA	MLB	24	406	64	.257	-0.9	CF(106): 3.3	-0.1
2019	NO	AAA	25	339	106	.356	2.3	CF(50): 4.4, RF(27): 5.1, LF(6): -0.6	2.2
2019	MIA	MLB	25	248	42	.253	1.5	CF(60): 6.4, RF(11): 0.7	-0.1
2020	MIA	MLB	26	112	83	.288	1.5	RF(31): -0.8, LF(21): 0.3, CF(7): 0.2	0.0
2021 FS	MIA	MLB	27	600	79	.291	0.3	RF 3, LF 0	0.5
2021 DC	MIA	MLB	27	159	79	.291	0.1	RF 1	0.0

Lewis Brinson, continued

Batted Ball Distribution

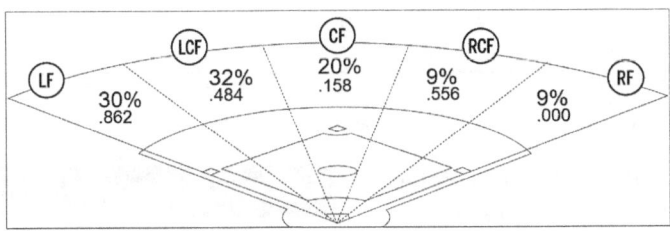

Strike Zone vs LHP   Strike Zone vs RHP

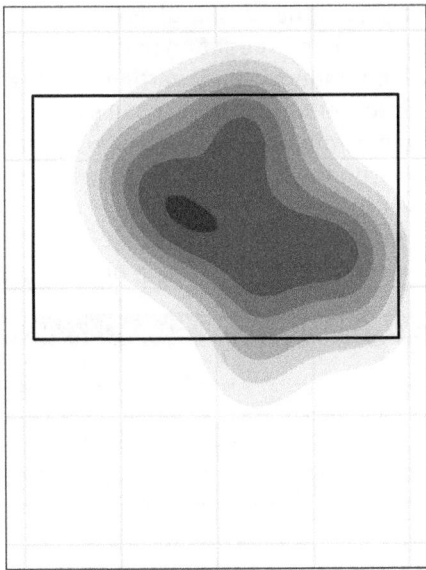

Francisco Cervelli C

Born: 03/06/86 Age: 35 Bats: R Throws: R
Height: 6'0" Weight: 220 Origin: International Free Agent, 2003

YEAR	TEAM	LVL	AGE	PA	R	2B	3B	HR	RBI	BB	K	SB	CS	AVG/OBP/SLG
2018	PIT	MLB	32	404	39	15	3	12	57	51	84	2	3	.259/.378/.431
2019	PIT	MLB	33	123	11	3	0	1	5	9	31	1	0	.193/.279/.248
2019	ATL	MLB	33	37	4	5	1	2	7	4	10	0	0	.281/.378/.688
2020	MIA	MLB	34	62	10	2	0	3	7	8	14	1	0	.245/.355/.453
2021 FS	MIA	MLB	35	600	63	20	1	13	60	69	146	5	3	.224/.335/.352

Comparables: Hank Foiles, Steve Yeager, Ray Noble

YEAR	TEAM	P. COUNT	FRM RUNS	BLK RUNS	THRW RUNS	TOT RUNS
2018	PIT	13280	-5.8	-1.1	0.6	-6.3
2019	ATL	835	0.0	-0.7	0.1	-0.6
2019	PIT	4334	0.0	-1.1	0.1	-1.0
2020	MIA	2102	-0.1	0.0	0.0	-0.1
2021	MIA	16650	-4.0	1.4	-0.2	-2.7
2021	MIA	16650	-4.0	-1.8	-0.2	-6.0

Cervelli retired in October to protect his health after suffering a season-ending concussion in August, his seventh reported concussion in the last decade. A year earlier, he'd briefly given up catching following his sixth head injury, which he told Jason Mackey of the *Pittsburgh Post-Gazette* had brought on panic attacks, violent mood swings, vertigo, and fogginess. For a short time in the mid-2010s, Cervelli emerged as baseball's newest two-way catching star, a venerable pitch framer with on-base skills who blossomed when he finally got a full-time job with the Pirates. The concussions robbed him of both skill and playing time over the past half-decade, and ultimately took away his ability to play at all, but even more worrisome are the potential long-term effects on Cervelli's health. We wish him all the best in his post-playing career.

YEAR	TEAM	LVL	AGE	PA	DRC+	BABIP	BRR	FRAA	WARP
2018	PIT	MLB	32	404	116	.308	0.7	C(94): -3.9, 1B(5): -0.1	2.4
2019	PIT	MLB	33	123	73	.260	-0.3	C(32): 0.3, 1B(1): -0.0	0.2
2019	ATL	MLB	33	37	94	.350	0.8	C(9): -0.6, 1B(2): -0.1	0.1
2020	MIA	MLB	34	62	101	.278	-0.6	C(16): 0.3	0.3
2021 FS	MIA	MLB	35	600	94	.287	-0.3	C -5, 1B 0	1.4

Francisco Cervelli, continued

Batted Ball Distribution

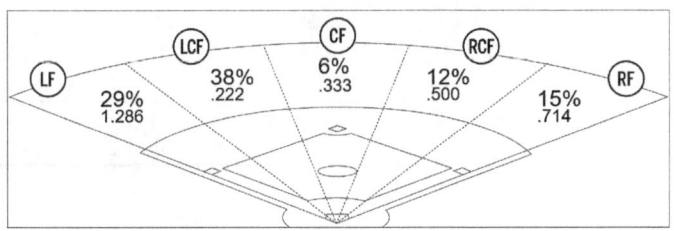

Strike Zone vs LHP   Strike Zone vs RHP

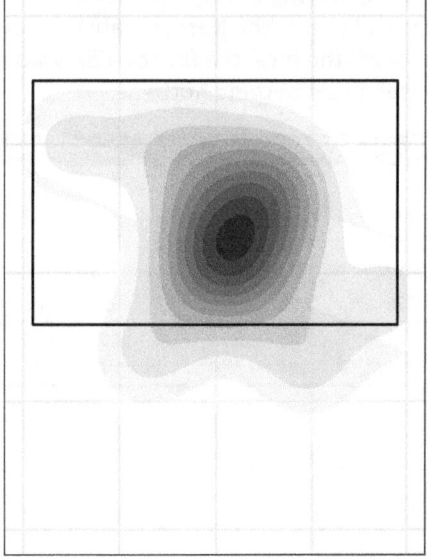

Miami Marlins 2021

Jazz Chisholm SS
Born: 02/01/98   Age: 23   Bats: L   Throws: R
Height: 5'11"   Weight: 184   Origin: International Free Agent, 2015

YEAR	TEAM	LVL	AGE	PA	R	2B	3B	HR	RBI	BB	K	SB	CS	AVG/OBP/SLG
2018	KC	LO-A	20	341	52	17	4	15	43	30	97	8	2	.244/.311/.472
2018	VIS	HI-A	20	160	27	6	2	10	27	9	52	9	2	.329/.369/.597
2019	JAX	AA	21	94	6	4	2	3	10	11	24	3	0	.284/.383/.494
2019	JXN	AA	21	364	51	6	5	18	44	41	123	13	4	.204/.305/.427
2020	MIA	MLB	22	62	8	1	1	2	6	5	19	2	2	.161/.242/.321
2021 FS	MIA	MLB	23	600	62	22	5	17	62	48	218	9	3	.206/.276/.361
2021 DC	MIA	MLB	23	248	25	9	2	7	25	20	90	3	2	.206/.276/.361

Comparables: Yu Chang, Cameron Maybin, Trevor Story

    Ideally, Chisholm's big-league debut wouldn't have involved being rushed into a late-season semi-regular role bouncing between shortstop, his natural position, and second. But 2020 wasn't ideal for anyone. Chisholm just wasn't prepared to hit major-league pitching after a season struggling to make contact at Double-A. He was overmatched, even while flashing the elite bat speed that makes him one of the top middle-infield prospects around. Even if it didn't quite go as planned, the Nassau native made history as the seventh Bahamian player to reach the bigs, the first of a new wave of impact prospects from one of baseball's emerging hotbeds.

YEAR	TEAM	LVL	AGE	PA	DRC+	BABIP	BRR	FRAA	WARP
2018	KC	LO-A	20	341	101	.303	-1.4	SS(75): -0.3	0.9
2018	VIS	HI-A	20	160	138	.443	0.5	SS(36): -0.7	0.9
2019	JAX	AA	21	94	103	.370	-0.5	SS(22): -1.8	0.4
2019	JXN	AA	21	364	108	.261	2.9	SS(88): -5.8	1.7
2020	MIA	MLB	22	62	74	.200	-0.4	2B(13): -1.7, SS(9): -0.1	-0.2
2021 FS	MIA	MLB	23	600	72	.307	1.0	SS -1, 2B -10	-1.3
2021 DC	MIA	MLB	23	248	72	.307	0.4	SS 0, 2B -4	-0.6

Jazz Chisholm, continued

Batted Ball Distribution

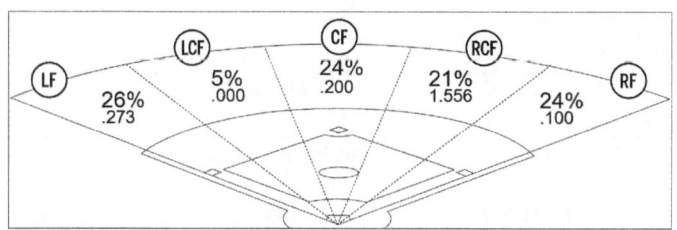

Strike Zone vs LHP   **Strike Zone vs RHP**

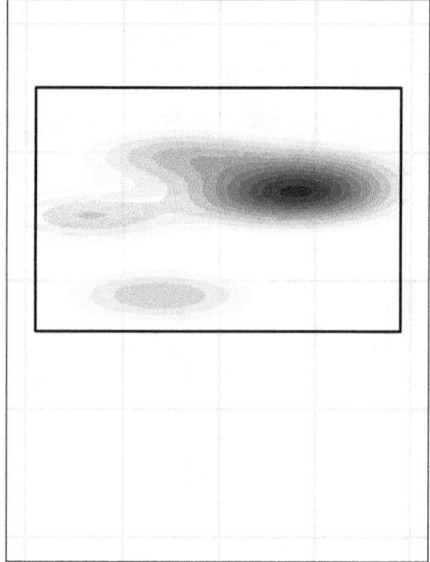

Miami Marlins 2021

Garrett Cooper 1B
Born: 12/25/90 Age: 30 Bats: R Throws: R
Height: 6'5" Weight: 235 Origin: Round 6, 2013 Draft (#182 overall)

YEAR	TEAM	LVL	AGE	PA	R	2B	3B	HR	RBI	BB	K	SB	CS	AVG/OBP/SLG
2018	NO	AAA	27	34	2	1	0	1	5	3	5	0	0	.300/.382/.433
2018	MIA	MLB	27	38	2	1	0	0	2	4	12	0	0	.212/.316/.242
2019	MIA	MLB	28	421	52	16	1	15	50	33	109	0	0	.281/.344/.446
2020	MIA	MLB	29	133	20	8	0	6	20	11	31	0	0	.283/.353/.500
2021 FS	MIA	MLB	30	600	75	27	1	23	76	49	154	0	1	.258/.329/.442
2021 DC	MIA	MLB	30	380	47	17	0	14	48	31	98	0	0	.258/.329/.442

Comparables: Brian Daubach, Andres Galarraga, Mark Trumbo

Cooper hit by far the biggest home run of his short career in Game 2 of the NL Wild Card Series, mashing a Yu Darvish hanging breaker over the ivy and out of the Friendly Confines of Wrigley. The dinger broke a 7th-inning scoreless tie and pushed the Marlins out of the three-game melee and into the divisional round. Cooper broke camp as the primary designated hitter, and for the first time in his Miami tenure, he wasn't forced to roam around the outfield in search of playing time that wasn't available at first base. Despite missing a month on the COVID-IL, he seems to have finally bridged the gap between Quad-A slugger and starting major-league player.

YEAR	TEAM	LVL	AGE	PA	DRC+	BABIP	BRR	FRAA	WARP
2018	NO	AAA	27	34	115	.333	-0.5	1B(5): 0.3, LF(4): 0.5	0.1
2018	MIA	MLB	27	38	66	.333	0.4	LF(6): 0.7, 1B(4): 1.1, RF(3): -0.1	0.1
2019	MIA	MLB	28	421	101	.355	-0.4	1B(73): -0.2, RF(31): 5.1	1.2
2020	MIA	MLB	29	133	110	.337	-0.8	1B(15): 0.6	0.4
2021 FS	MIA	MLB	30	600	112	.321	-0.9	1B 0, LF 0	1.9
2021 DC	MIA	MLB	30	380	112	.321	-0.6	1B 0	1.1

Garrett Cooper, continued

Batted Ball Distribution

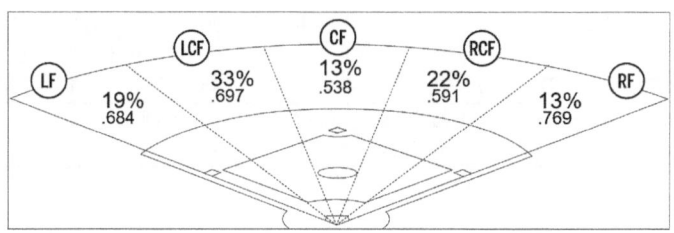

Strike Zone vs LHP   Strike Zone vs RHP

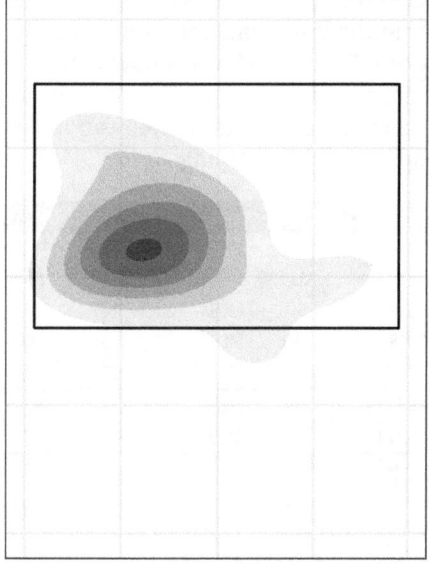

Miami Marlins 2021

Corey Dickerson OF

Born: 05/22/89   Age: 32   Bats: L   Throws: R
Height: 6'1"   Weight: 200   Origin: Round 8, 2010 Draft (#260 overall)

YEAR	TEAM	LVL	AGE	PA	R	2B	3B	HR	RBI	BB	K	SB	CS	AVG/OBP/SLG
2018	PIT	MLB	29	533	65	35	7	13	55	21	80	8	3	.300/.330/.474
2019	IND	AAA	30	38	4	1	0	0	4	3	8	0	0	.182/.237/.212
2019	PIT	MLB	30	142	20	18	0	4	25	13	23	1	0	.315/.373/.551
2019	PHI	MLB	30	137	13	10	2	8	34	3	33	0	0	.293/.307/.579
2020	MIA	MLB	31	210	25	5	1	7	17	15	35	1	1	.258/.311/.402
2021 FS	MIA	MLB	32	600	71	28	3	19	68	35	129	4	2	.245/.293/.412
2021 DC	MIA	MLB	32	488	57	23	2	15	55	29	105	3	2	.245/.293/.412

Comparables: Alfonso Soriano, Starling Marte, Yoenis Céspedes

One of the most consistent hitters in baseball, Dickerson put up his sixth consecutive season with a DRC+ between 100 and 109 for his fifth different team in that span. He took his talents to South Beach as the nominal big fish in Miami's offseason consignment store shopping, signing a two-year, $17.5 million bargain. After a typically steady performance in the regular season, he delivered one of the biggest hits in recent franchise history when he bopped a three-run go-ahead homer against the Cubs in Game 1 of the NL Wild Card Series. Dickerson has his flaws—he can't hit lefties well and doesn't get on base quite as much as you'd like—but adding a few average-caliber regulars like him lifted the Marlins out of their rebuild a year or two ahead of schedule. More teams should try trying.

YEAR	TEAM	LVL	AGE	PA	DRC+	BABIP	BRR	FRAA	WARP
2018	PIT	MLB	29	533	105	.333	-4.1	LF(124): 10.7	2.4
2019	IND	AAA	30	38	60	.222	0.2	LF(7): 0.6	0.0
2019	PIT	MLB	30	142	107	.353	-0.1	LF(33): -0.7	0.5
2019	PHI	MLB	30	137	105	.333	-3.1	LF(32): -1.2	0.0
2020	MIA	MLB	31	210	99	.283	1.0	LF(46): -3.0, RF(1): -0.0	0.3
2021 FS	MIA	MLB	32	600	90	.286	-0.1	LF 2, RF 0	0.9
2021 DC	MIA	MLB	32	488	90	.286	-0.1	LF 1	0.7

Corey Dickerson, continued

Batted Ball Distribution

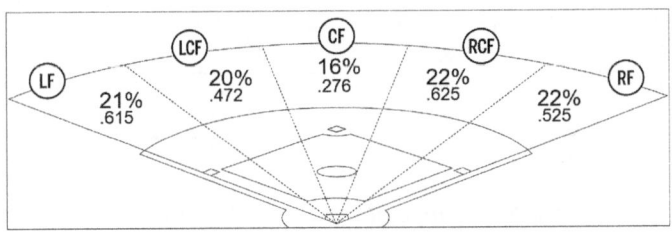

Strike Zone vs LHP   Strike Zone vs RHP

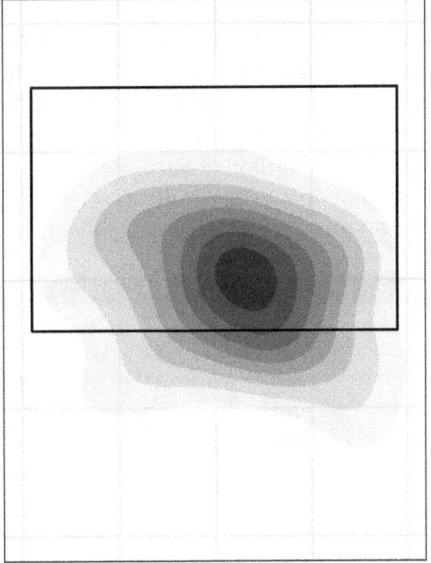

Starling Marte CF

Born: 10/09/88   Age: 32   Bats: R   Throws: R
Height: 6'1"   Weight: 195   Origin: International Free Agent, 2007

YEAR	TEAM	LVL	AGE	PA	R	2B	3B	HR	RBI	BB	K	SB	CS	AVG/OBP/SLG
2018	PIT	MLB	29	606	81	32	5	20	72	35	109	33	14	.277/.327/.460
2019	PIT	MLB	30	586	97	31	6	23	82	25	94	25	6	.295/.342/.503
2020	MIA	MLB	31	112	13	6	0	4	13	2	22	5	0	.245/.286/.415
2020	ARI	MLB	31	138	23	8	1	2	14	10	19	5	2	.311/.384/.443
2021 FS	MIA	MLB	32	600	76	27	3	17	72	31	119	35	11	.271/.331/.430
2021 DC	MIA	MLB	32	602	76	27	3	17	72	31	119	35	11	.271/.331/.430

Comparables: Al Martin, Jeffrey Leonard, Matt Diaz

Consider Marte as representative of the game of baseball and state of things more broadly in 2020. He opened the year by getting traded to Arizona for a pair of high-upside, intriguing prospects—the quality of which reflected not only Marte's on-field prowess but the affordable team option on him for 2021, as well. He suffered unfathomable personal loss during baseball's interregnum when his wife Noelia Brazoban suffered a fatal heart attack in May. He decided to play once baseball returned in late July, but found himself changing teams once again at the deadline, that affordable option now rendered as a burden due to Arizona's so-called economic headwinds. Marte was a salve for an experienced and strikeout-prone outfield in Miami and helped spur the team to their playoff entry, though he missed most of the postseason with a broken finger. The Marlins rewarded him and themselves by exercising their option for next year. In a year where March stretched on for years, Marte's 61 games played in a 60-game schedule was truly emblematic.

YEAR	TEAM	LVL	AGE	PA	DRC+	BABIP	BRR	FRAA	WARP
2018	PIT	MLB	29	606	107	.312	0.1	CF(139): 7.0	3.4
2019	PIT	MLB	30	586	107	.319	3.9	CF(130): 2.3	3.4
2020	MIA	MLB	31	112	98	.275	0.1	CF(28): -1.8	0.2
2020	ARI	MLB	31	138	100	.353	1.0	CF(33): -0.6, LF(1): 0.0	0.4
2021 FS	MIA	MLB	32	600	109	.318	2.9	CF 4, LF 0	3.4
2021 DC	MIA	MLB	32	602	109	.318	2.9	CF 4	3.3

Starling Marte, continued

Batted Ball Distribution

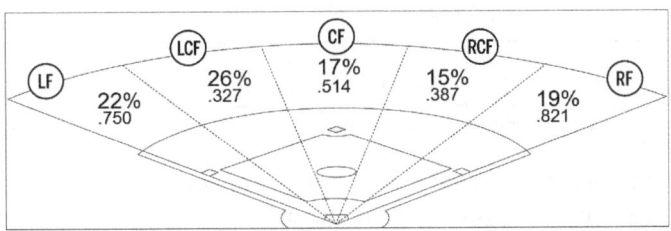

Strike Zone vs LHP   **Strike Zone vs RHP**

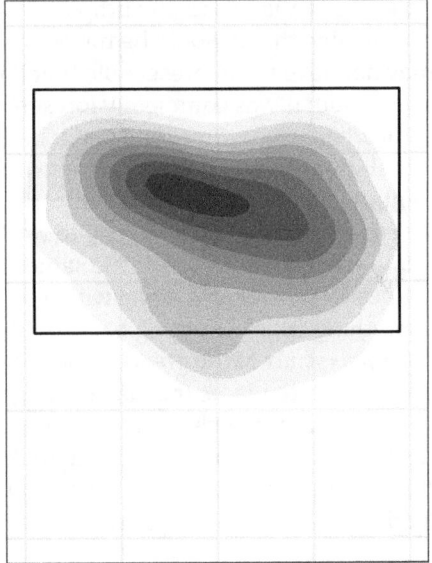

Miami Marlins 2021

Miguel Rojas SS

Born: 02/24/89 Age: 32 Bats: R Throws: R
Height: 6'0" Weight: 188 Origin: International Free Agent, 2005

YEAR	TEAM	LVL	AGE	PA	R	2B	3B	HR	RBI	BB	K	SB	CS	AVG/OBP/SLG
2018	MIA	MLB	29	528	44	13	0	11	53	24	69	6	3	.252/.297/.346
2019	MIA	MLB	30	526	52	29	1	5	46	32	61	9	5	.284/.331/.379
2020	MIA	MLB	31	143	20	10	1	4	20	16	18	5	1	.304/.392/.496
2021 FS	MIA	MLB	32	600	67	28	1	11	58	42	86	7	4	.260/.323/.381
2021 DC	MIA	MLB	32	524	58	25	1	10	51	36	75	6	3	.260/.323/.381

Comparables: Kevin Elster, Larry Brown, Marco Scutaro

Far too many people in power around the world abdicated their responsibility in 2020, in baseball and beyond. The abdication of power by Major League Baseball and commissioner Rob Manfred enveloped the entire season, starting when the league frittered away weeks and weeks of time and planning in a futile attempt to pay players less than pro rata. It continued to the very end, when the league failed to keep a COVID-positive player away from the on-field celebration at the end of the World Series. The worst example was in the middle, in the handling of Miami's team outbreak in late July. It may not have been foreseeable that it would be the Marlins who would have an outbreak, and it may not have been foreseeable that it would be on the very first weekend of the season, but it was completely foreseeable that an outbreak would happen somewhere, sometime. And Major League Baseball had no real response for it, initially leaving the decision about whether or not to forge ahead in the face of multiple positive tests up to the Marlins players. There were no protocols on when to hit pause, on how long to wait, on what to do; just an operational manual filled with much of the same virus theater that has permeated all aspects of our society, along with a broader idea that if the players did everything "right," nothing bad would happen. Of course, since everything in baseball is part of the greater labor fight now, when things went wrong, the answer was to blame the players for getting sick. It may have been Miguel Rojas who led Miami's decision to play on July 26th as the unofficial team leader, but it never should've been his call to make. Rojas was ultimately one of over a dozen Marlins to test positive; he would homer in his return four weeks later and lead the team to the playoffs.

YEAR	TEAM	LVL	AGE	PA	DRC+	BABIP	BRR	FRAA	WARP
2018	MIA	MLB	29	528	90	.272	-2.5	SS(83): 5.4, 1B(49): -0.3, 3B(39): -1.0	1.6
2019	MIA	MLB	30	526	93	.313	-1.7	SS(125): -4.8, 1B(6): -0.1, 2B(3): -0.1	1.4
2020	MIA	MLB	31	143	123	.330	-0.6	SS(39): 6.4, 1B(1): -0.0, 3B(1): 0.0	1.5
2021 FS	MIA	MLB	32	600	95	.292	-0.2	SS 1, 1B 0	1.4
2021 DC	MIA	MLB	32	524	95	.292	-0.2	SS 1	1.3

Miguel Rojas, continued

Batted Ball Distribution

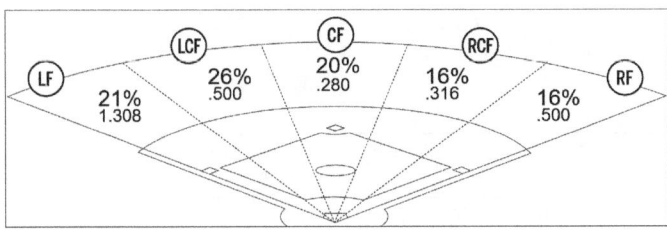

Strike Zone vs LHP   **Strike Zone vs RHP**

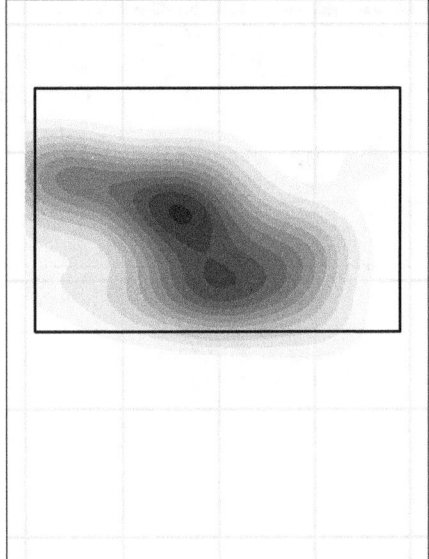

Miami Marlins 2021

Magneuris Sierra CF
Born: 04/07/96   Age: 25   Bats: L   Throws: L
Height: 5'11"   Weight: 178   Origin: International Free Agent, 2012

YEAR	TEAM	LVL	AGE	PA	R	2B	3B	HR	RBI	BB	K	SB	CS	AVG/OBP/SLG
2018	NO	AAA	22	367	48	12	5	2	17	13	73	14	5	.260/.287/.341
2018	MIA	MLB	22	156	10	3	0	0	7	6	39	3	2	.190/.222/.211
2019	JAX	AA	23	197	21	8	2	1	7	13	32	7	1	.282/.337/.365
2019	NO	AAA	23	352	56	11	7	6	21	15	58	26	10	.271/.304/.399
2019	MIA	MLB	23	42	5	1	1	0	1	2	7	3	3	.350/.381/.425
2020	MIA	MLB	24	53	8	3	1	0	7	5	9	4	1	.250/.333/.364
2021 FS	MIA	MLB	25	600	59	21	6	7	50	31	142	16	8	.236/.280/.333
2021 DC	MIA	MLB	25	97	9	3	0	1	8	5	22	2	1	.236/.280/.333

Comparables: Brady Anderson, Eddie Miller, Joey Gathright

Sierra might finally be settling in as a nifty slash-and-burn fourth outfielder, which is an upgrade from the past few seasons where it looked like his offensive profile had been slashed and burned.

YEAR	TEAM	LVL	AGE	PA	DRC+	BABIP	BRR	FRAA	WARP
2018	NO	AAA	22	367	60	.322	3.2	CF(81): 5.8, RF(1): 0.7	0.2
2018	MIA	MLB	22	156	39	.259	-0.4	CF(32): -0.3, RF(19): -0.1	-0.8
2019	JAX	AA	23	197	109	.338	1.8	CF(21): 0.7, RF(15): 4.2, LF(4): 1.7	1.6
2019	NO	AAA	23	352	61	.312	3.7	CF(32): -0.7, LF(24): -1.4, RF(23): 1.5	-0.3
2019	MIA	MLB	23	42	81	.424	-0.7	CF(9): 3.3, RF(5): 0.4	0.3
2020	MIA	MLB	24	53	102	.306	-0.3	CF(11): 1.4, LF(5): 0.8, RF(4): 0.1	0.3
2021 FS	MIA	MLB	25	600	66	.303	2.0	RF 5, CF 3	0.1
2021 DC	MIA	MLB	25	97	66	.303	0.3	RF 1, CF 0	0.0

Magneuris Sierra, continued

Batted Ball Distribution

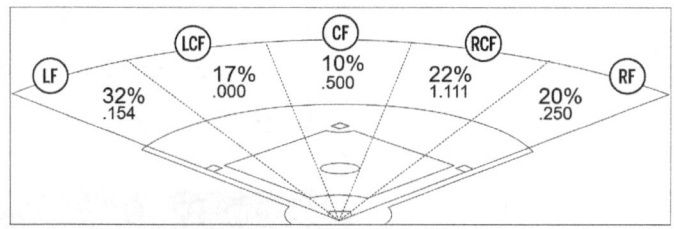

Strike Zone vs LHP   **Strike Zone vs RHP**

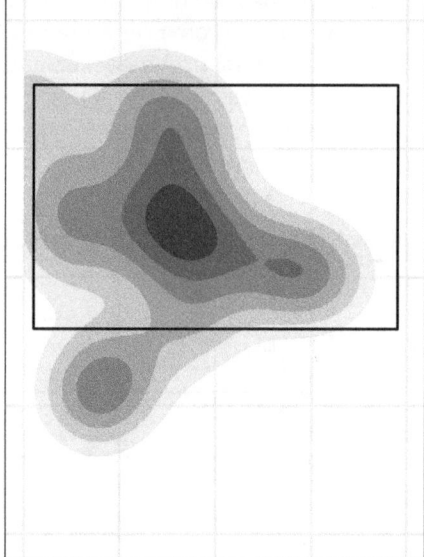

Miami Marlins 2021

Chad Wallach C

Born: 11/04/91   Age: 29   Bats: R   Throws: R
Height: 6'2"   Weight: 246   Origin: Round 5, 2013 Draft (#142 overall)

YEAR	TEAM	LVL	AGE	PA	R	2B	3B	HR	RBI	BB	K	SB	CS	AVG/OBP/SLG
2018	NO	AAA	26	174	20	7	0	3	16	20	47	0	1	.224/.324/.333
2018	MIA	MLB	26	52	4	1	0	1	5	4	23	0	0	.178/.275/.267
2019	MIA	MLB	27	54	4	3	0	1	3	6	12	0	0	.250/.333/.375
2020	MIA	MLB	28	48	4	3	0	1	6	3	12	0	0	.227/.277/.364
2021 FS	MIA	MLB	29	600	66	21	1	19	63	54	180	0	1	.211/.294/.362
2021 DC	MIA	MLB	29	213	23	7	0	6	22	19	64	0	0	.211/.294/.362

Comparables: Juan Brito, Guillermo Quiroz, Max Stassi

Catching admittedly remains a bit of a mystery box to baseball analysts, even with pitch framing solved. The Marlins love what Wallach brings to the table as a staff leader and game caller—soft factors we can't quantify well—so much so that they ran him out in every postseason game. From one vantage point, he's a generic no-hit backup catcher with a decent but unspectacular glove and a well-respected last name. But he keeps moving up in the world despite that, from waiver claim to up-and-down third catcher to backup to playoff starter. Perhaps his virtue falls in the presently unquantifiable space between.

YEAR	TEAM	P. COUNT	FRM RUNS	BLK RUNS	THRW RUNS	TOT RUNS
2018	MIA	2036	2.2	0.3	0.1	2.6
2019	MIA	1947	0.4	-1.5	0.0	-1.1
2020	MIA	1950	0.0	0.2	0.0	0.2
2021	MIA	8418	1.9	1.1	0.2	3.2
2021	MIA	8418	1.9	0.7	0.2	2.8

YEAR	TEAM	LVL	AGE	PA	DRC+	BABIP	BRR	FRAA	WARP
2018	NO	AAA	26	174	83	.300	-2.6	C(40): 8.1	0.8
2018	MIA	MLB	26	52	54	.333	0.1	C(14): 2.6	0.3
2019	MIA	MLB	27	54	96	.314	-0.1	C(14): -0.7	0.2
2020	MIA	MLB	28	48	81	.290	-0.4	C(15): -0.3	0.0
2021 FS	MIA	MLB	29	600	80	.279	-0.8	C 6	1.5
2021 DC	MIA	MLB	29	213	80	.279	-0.3	C 3	0.6

Chad Wallach, continued

Batted Ball Distribution

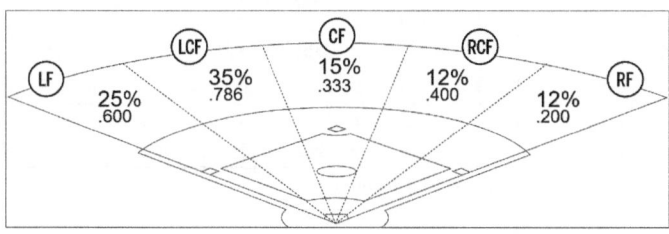

Strike Zone vs LHP **Strike Zone vs RHP**

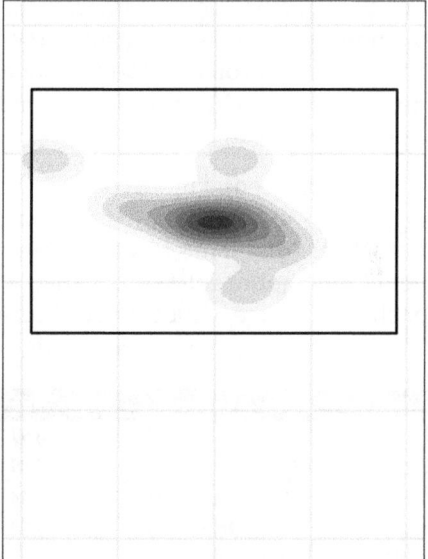

Miami Marlins 2021

Sandy Alcantara RHP
Born: 09/07/95 Age: 25 Bats: R Throws: R
Height: 6'5" Weight: 200 Origin: International Free Agent, 2013

YEAR	TEAM	LVL	AGE	W	L	SV	G	GS	IP	H	HR	BB/9	K/9	K	GB%	BABIP
2018	JUP	HI-A	22	0	0	0	3	3	11[1]	10	0	4.0	6.4	8	61.8%	.294
2018	NO	AAA	22	6	3	0	19	19	115[2]	107	10	3.0	6.8	88	48.7%	.284
2018	MIA	MLB	22	2	3	0	6	6	34	25	3	6.1	7.9	30	47.3%	.256
2019	MIA	MLB	23	6	14	0	32	32	197[1]	179	23	3.7	6.9	151	44.1%	.274
2020	MIA	MLB	24	3	2	0	7	7	42	35	4	3.2	8.4	39	49.6%	.277
2021 FS	MIA	MLB	25	9	8	0	26	26	150	142	20	4.2	8.2	137	46.0%	.290
2021 DC	MIA	MLB	25	10	9	0	27	27	159.7	151	21	4.2	8.2	145	46.0%	.290

Comparables: Lucas Giolito, Tyler Mahle, Luis Severino

Alcantara may never turn out to be the ace that his velocity and stuff portends, but he is plenty good in his current form. He's already driven past many of the roadblocks that force hard-throwing starting prospects into the 'pen. Alcantara is durable and turning into quite the innings eater, missed time in 2020 due to COVID notwithstanding. He's now a five-pitch starter, throwing a two-seam fastball, four-seam fastball, slider, changeup and curveball. And he pounds the strike zone, belying earlier command concerns from his days as a top prospect. If you can throw enough innings, pitches and strikes to stay in the rotation, and you have an arm as good as Alcantara's, you're not that far off from a high-end outcome.

Alcantara needs a more consistent swing-and-miss offering to take the last big step towards the top of the rotation. He started getting more whiffs on his fastball in 2020 thanks to a tick more heat but it remains to be seen if that will hold throughout a full season. There's no true out pitch at present, just a variety of above-average or plus that will occasionally flash bigger. Until that happens, he's "only" going to be a mid-rotation stalwart.

YEAR	TEAM	LVL	AGE	WHIP	ERA	DRA-	WARP	MPH	FB%	WHF	CSP
2018	JUP	HI-A	22	1.32	3.97	132	-0.1				
2018	NO	AAA	22	1.25	3.89	89	1.8				
2018	MIA	MLB	22	1.41	3.44	124	-0.1	98.0	60.0%	27.1%	
2019	MIA	MLB	23	1.32	3.88	93	2.6	97.7	57.0%	23.8%	
2020	MIA	MLB	24	1.19	3.00	85	0.7	98.4	60.0%	24.1%	
2021 FS	MIA	MLB	25	1.42	4.46	101	1.3	97.9	57.9%	24.1%	49.3%
2021 DC	MIA	MLB	25	1.42	4.46	101	1.4	97.9	57.9%	24.1%	49.3%

Sandy Alcantara, continued

Pitch Shape vs LHH

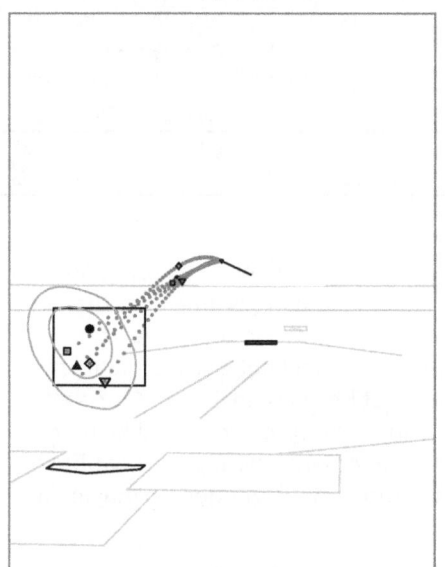

Pitch Shape vs RHH

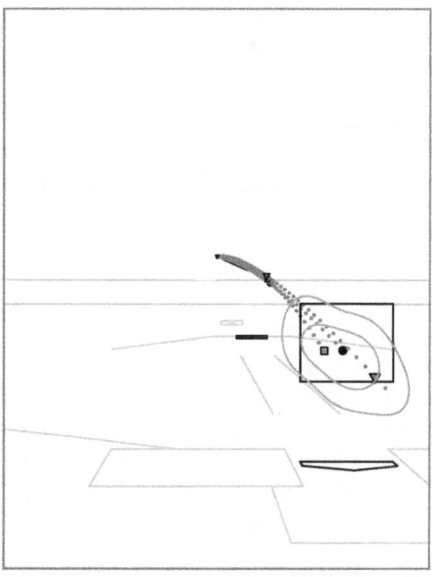

Type	Frequency	Velocity	H Movement	V Movement
● Fastball	24.9%	97 [114]	-8.5 [91]	-12.7 [107]
□ Sinker	35.0%	96.4 [120]	-15.2 [84]	-19.4 [104]
▲ Changeup	10.0%	90.2 [120]	-14.6 [85]	-26.9 [102]
▽ Slider	22.7%	87.4 [116]	2.3 [89]	-30.3 [110]
◇ Curveball	7.4%	81.9 [113]	5.6 [92]	-40.4 [118]

Miami Marlins 2021

Anthony Bass   RHP
Born: 11/01/87   Age: 33   Bats: R   Throws: R
Height: 6'2"   Weight: 200   Origin: Round 5, 2008 Draft (#165 overall)

YEAR	TEAM	LVL	AGE	W	L	SV	G	GS	IP	H	HR	BB/9	K/9	K	GB%	BABIP
2018	IOW	AAA	30	0	3	3	27	0	32	34	3	1.7	7.0	25	51.0%	.310
2018	CHC	MLB	30	0	0	0	16	0	15^1	18	1	1.8	8.2	14	53.3%	.386
2019	LOU	AAA	31	1	1	9	19	0	20^1	13	1	2.7	8.4	19	52.7%	.222
2019	SEA	MLB	31	2	4	5	44	0	48	30	5	3.2	8.1	43	53.1%	.207
2020	TOR	MLB	32	2	3	7	26	0	25^2	17	2	3.2	7.4	21	61.4%	.224
2021 FS	MIA	MLB	33	2	2	21	57	0	50	45	5	3.2	8.1	44	52.6%	.282
2021 DC	MIA	MLB	33	3	3	21	66	0	57.7	52	6	3.2	8.1	51	52.6%	.282

Comparables: Jeremy Affeldt, Jeremy Jeffress, Tommy Hunter

Bass appeared in more games than any other Jays pitcher, and for good reason. The journeyman, appearing on the sixth team of his nine-year major league career, threw more sinkers and sliders than ever before, generating whiffs and groundballs at career-high rates. Bass is still not a strikeout artist, and he was certainly not unhittable in 2020. But he was consistent: Game after game, Bass could be relied upon for a solid inning-plus of work, and he made very few appearances that could qualify as meltdowns. Perhaps the symbol of this relief corps, Bass was a pre-season afterthought who ended up playing a critical role in the Jays' postseason run.

YEAR	TEAM	LVL	AGE	WHIP	ERA	DRA-	WARP	MPH	FB%	WHF	CSP
2018	IOW	AAA	30	1.25	3.38	75	0.6				
2018	CHC	MLB	30	1.37	2.93	106	0.0	95.6	68.4%	20.8%	
2019	LOU	AAA	31	0.93	2.21	55	0.7				
2019	SEA	MLB	31	0.98	3.56	70	1.0	97.0	52.7%	27.9%	
2020	TOR	MLB	32	1.01	3.51	84	0.4	96.4	54.2%	28.0%	
2021 FS	MIA	MLB	33	1.26	3.49	85	0.7	96.6	54.6%	27.3%	43.6%
2021 DC	MIA	MLB	33	1.26	3.49	85	0.8	96.6	54.6%	27.3%	43.6%

Anthony Bass, continued

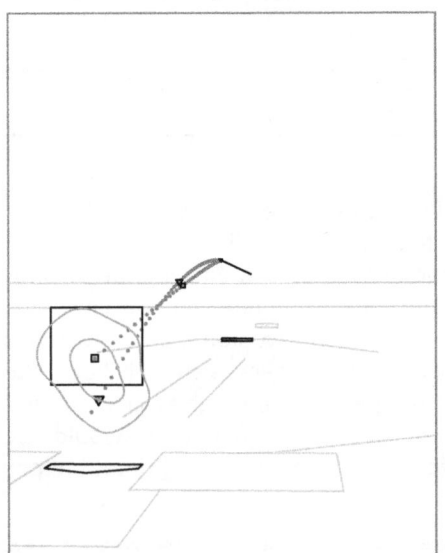 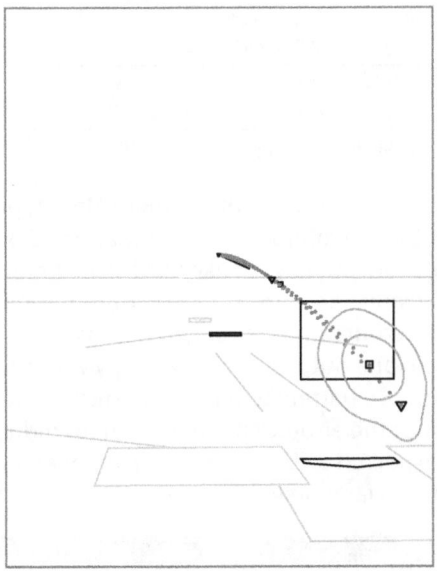

Pitch Shape vs LHH | Pitch Shape vs RHH

Type	Frequency	Velocity	H Movement	V Movement
☐ Sinker	52.8%	94.8 [112]	-11.7 [110]	-15 [118]
✕ Splitter	6.6%	86.5 [106]	-7.2 [103]	-21.2 [127]
▽ Slider	38.1%	85.9 [109]	4.3 [97]	-33.7 [100]

Richard Bleier LHP
Born: 04/16/87 Age: 34 Bats: L Throws: L
Height: 6'3" Weight: 215 Origin: Round 6, 2008 Draft (#183 overall)

YEAR	TEAM	LVL	AGE	W	L	SV	G	GS	IP	H	HR	BB/9	K/9	K	GB%	BABIP
2018	BAL	MLB	31	3	0	0	31	0	32²	36	0	1.1	4.1	15	57.5%	.319
2019	BAL	MLB	32	3	0	4	53	1	55¹	65	6	1.3	4.9	30	59.6%	.317
2020	MIA	MLB	33	1	1	0	21	0	16²	14	0	2.2	5.9	11	70.6%	.275
2021 FS	MIA	MLB	34	2	2	0	57	0	50	53	5	2.1	5.8	32	60.6%	.297
2021 DC	MIA	MLB	34	2	2	0	53	0	57.7	61	6	2.1	5.8	37	60.6%	.297

Comparables: Tommy Hunter, Chris Rusin, Luis García

Bleier was a reinforcement Marlin, picked up from the Orioles during the COVID layoff for a PTBNL that turned out to be a rookie-ball flier. Baltimore general manager Mike Elias said Miami had prior interest in Bleier, though, and he hung around as a setup option even after the cavalry returned. He's a no-true-outcomes leftballer, hurling up a mix of low-velocity slop that rarely strikes anyone out, while being stingy with the walks and homers—generally hoping to induce batters to hit 'em where they are. He's just good enough against righties that the anti-LOOGY rule changes didn't kill his career. Honestly, one would have expected a "break glass in case of emergency" pickup out of the Orioles bullpen to do far worse.

YEAR	TEAM	LVL	AGE	WHIP	ERA	DRA-	WARP	MPH	FB%	WHF	CSP
2018	BAL	MLB	31	1.22	1.93	113	-0.1	89.9	60.8%	19.1%	
2019	BAL	MLB	32	1.32	5.37	107	0.1	90.8	64.7%	17.1%	
2020	MIA	MLB	33	1.08	2.16	65	0.5	90.4	53.2%	17.0%	
2021 FS	MIA	MLB	34	1.30	4.01	96	0.3	90.6	61.2%	17.4%	51.9%
2021 DC	MIA	MLB	34	1.30	4.01	96	0.4	90.6	61.2%	17.4%	51.9%

Richard Bleier, continued

Pitch Shape vs LHH

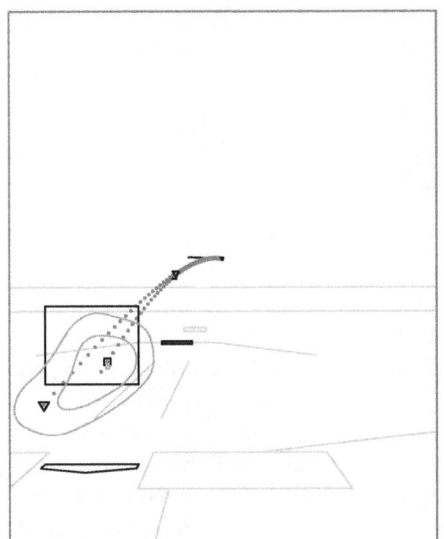

Pitch Shape vs RHH

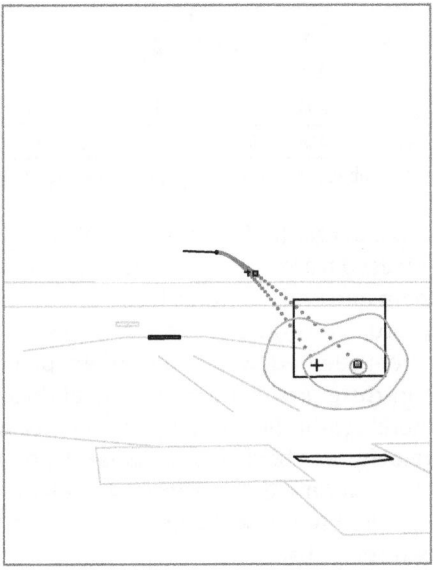

Type	Frequency	Velocity	H Movement	V Movement
☐ Sinker	50.0%	89 [82]	13.4 [98]	-26.3 [81]
+ Cutter	16.7%	88.1 [99]	0.8 [82]	-25.2 [96]
▲ Changeup	5.4%	82.9 [91]	14.8 [84]	-29.8 [94]
▽ Slider	23.9%	78.8 [77]	-4.6 [97]	-40.8 [79]

Brad Boxberger RHP

Born: 05/27/88   Age: 33   Bats: R   Throws: R
Height: 5'10"   Weight: 211   Origin: Round 1, 2009 Draft (#43 overall)

YEAR	TEAM	LVL	AGE	W	L	SV	G	GS	IP	H	HR	BB/9	K/9	K	GB%	BABIP
2018	ARI	MLB	30	3	7	32	60	0	53^1	44	9	5.4	12.0	71	45.8%	.292
2019	HBG	AA	31	1	1	1	8	0	8^2	6	0	3.1	11.4	11	38.1%	.286
2019	LOU	AAA	31	0	0	0	5	0	5^1	10	2	8.4	13.5	8	16.7%	.500
2019	KC	MLB	31	1	3	1	29	0	26^2	25	3	5.7	9.1	27	39.0%	.297
2020	MIA	MLB	32	1	0	0	23	0	18	17	3	4.0	9.0	18	50.0%	.286
2021 FS	MIA	MLB	33	2	2	0	57	0	50	43	6	4.4	9.6	53	42.4%	.285

Comparables: Mike Dunn, Jeremy Jeffress, Santiago Casilla

Boxberger looked utterly cooked at the end of 2019, a season in which he was released from not only Kansas City's major-league club, but Cincinnati's Triple-A team and Washington's Double-A team. It wasn't a tough diagnosis: He could ill afford a full grade of command, nor either of the ticks he lost on his heater. His career seemed, well, done. Miami picked him up for a no-risk look-see on a late non-roster invite, the type of deal thrown at former All-Star closers to see if there's something to fix. In a bit of a surprise, some juice remained. Boxberger's velocity was back and he made the team, quickly establishing himself as The Eighth-Inning Guy, performing well during the regular season and playoff run. He might not be a closer anymore and he's certainly not an All-Star, but it's not a bad second act.

YEAR	TEAM	LVL	AGE	WHIP	ERA	DRA-	WARP	MPH	FB%	WHF	CSP
2018	ARI	MLB	30	1.43	4.39	114	-0.1	93.4	66.3%	27.1%	
2019	HBG	AA	31	1.04	1.04	71	0.1				
2019	LOU	AAA	31	2.81	11.81	179	-0.1				
2019	KC	MLB	31	1.57	5.40	126	-0.2	91.6	47.0%	29.0%	
2020	MIA	MLB	32	1.39	3.00	83	0.3	94.1	55.2%	24.2%	
2021 FS	MIA	MLB	33	1.36	3.95	91	0.5	93.1	56.1%	26.7%	47.2%

Brad Boxberger, continued

Pitch Shape vs LHH	Pitch Shape vs RHH
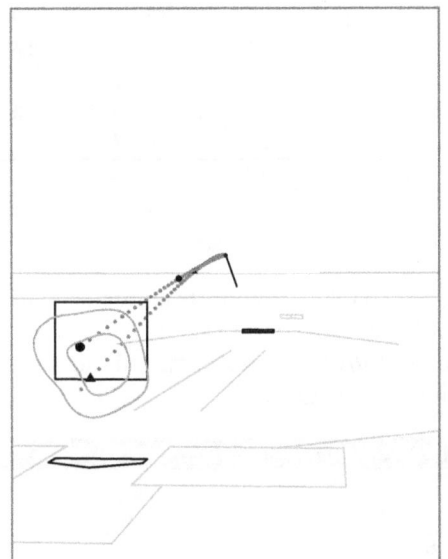	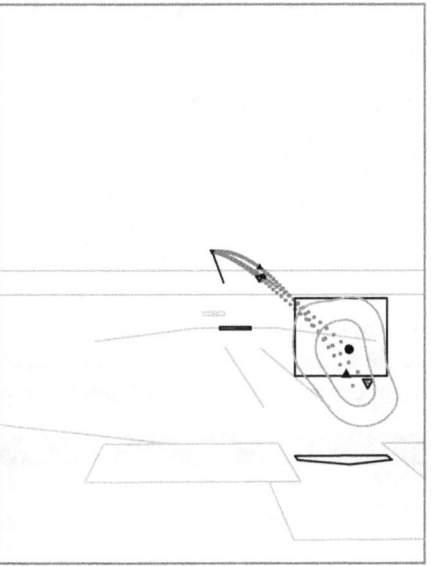

Type	Frequency	Velocity	H Movement	V Movement
● Fastball	55.2%	92.6 [100]	-5.1 [108]	-12.7 [107]
▲ Changeup	26.6%	81.4 [85]	-13 [93]	-32.6 [86]
▽ Slider	17.6%	88.4 [120]	4.4 [97]	-22.9 [131]

Miami Marlins 2021

Daniel Castano LHP
Born: 09/17/94   Age: 26   Bats: L   Throws: L
Height: 6'3"   Weight: 231   Origin: Round 19, 2016 Draft (#586 overall)

YEAR	TEAM	LVL	AGE	W	L	SV	G	GS	IP	H	HR	BB/9	K/9	K	GB%	BABIP
2018	MRL	ROK	23	0	1	0	2	1	9	10	0	0.0	8.0	8	58.6%	.345
2018	GBO	LO-A	23	4	3	0	8	8	50	48	10	0.7	9.4	52	62.0%	.288
2018	JUP	HI-A	23	5	8	0	14	14	76	95	3	2.8	6.6	56	54.2%	.359
2019	JUP	HI-A	24	0	2	0	12	0	33	33	2	1.9	8.5	31	61.8%	.316
2019	JAX	AA	24	7	2	0	18	11	86	82	2	1.7	7.6	73	48.5%	.308
2020	MIA	MLB	25	1	2	0	7	6	29^2	30	3	3.3	3.6	12	46.6%	.270
2021 FS	MIA	MLB	26	2	3	0	57	0	50	53	7	2.6	6.2	34	45.8%	.294
2021 DC	MIA	MLB	26	6	3	0	45	4	57.7	62	8	2.6	6.2	40	45.8%	.294

Comparables: Gregory Soto, Cody Stashak, Joe Palumbo

Soft-tossing lefty Castano was called upon to take a few starts in August when nobody else in the organization could. While his ERA sparkled enough to get some additional work later in the season, his DRA and peripherals tell the story of an overmatched Quad-A pitcher walking a very tight rope.

YEAR	TEAM	LVL	AGE	WHIP	ERA	DRA-	WARP	MPH	FB%	WHF	CSP
2018	MRL	ROK	23	1.11	4.00						
2018	GBO	LO-A	23	1.04	2.70	79	0.8				
2018	JUP	HI-A	23	1.57	4.74	81	1.2				
2019	JUP	HI-A	24	1.21	3.82	96	0.0				
2019	JAX	AA	24	1.14	3.35	94	0.3				
2020	MIA	MLB	25	1.38	3.03	127	-0.2	92.0	50.2%	19.7%	
2021 FS	MIA	MLB	26	1.37	4.53	106	0.1	92.0	50.2%	19.7%	50.6%
2021 DC	MIA	MLB	26	1.37	4.53	106	0.3	92.0	50.2%	19.7%	50.6%

Daniel Castano, continued

Pitch Shape vs LHH

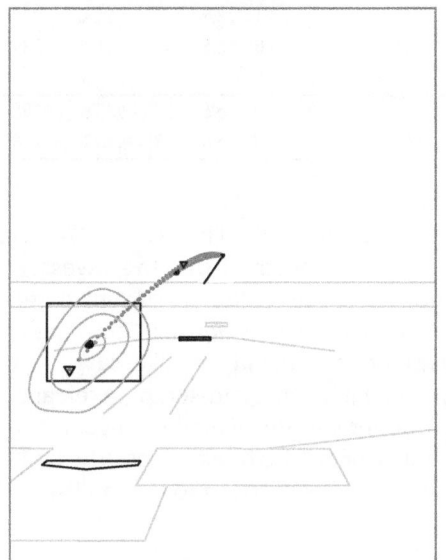

Pitch Shape vs RHH

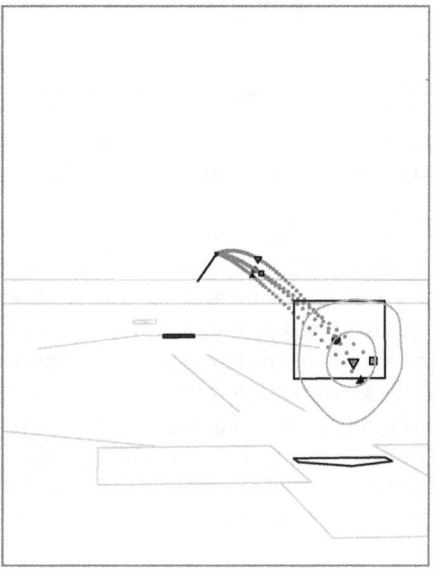

Type	Frequency	Velocity	H Movement	V Movement
● Fastball	32.9%	89.9 [91]	2.7 [119]	-20 [86]
□ Sinker	17.3%	88.3 [79]	8.3 [135]	-22.4 [94]
▲ Changeup	24.1%	82 [88]	10.2 [108]	-24.2 [109]
▽ Slider	25.7%	79.6 [81]	-6.5 [105]	-38.9 [85]

Adam Cimber   RHP

Born: 08/15/90   Age: 30   Bats: R   Throws: R
Height: 6'3"   Weight: 195   Origin: Round 9, 2013 Draft (#268 overall)

YEAR	TEAM	LVL	AGE	W	L	SV	G	GS	IP	H	HR	BB/9	K/9	K	GB%	BABIP
2018	SD	MLB	27	3	5	0	42	0	48^1	42	2	1.9	9.5	51	51.9%	.317
2018	CLE	MLB	27	0	3	0	28	0	20	26	3	3.1	3.1	7	66.2%	.329
2019	CLE	MLB	28	6	3	1	68	0	56^2	56	6	3.0	6.5	41	55.0%	.289
2020	CLE	MLB	29	0	1	0	14	0	11^1	13	1	1.6	4.0	5	52.4%	.293
2021 FS	MIA	MLB	30	2	2	0	57	0	50	51	5	2.0	6.8	37	52.7%	.298
2021 DC	MIA	MLB	30	2	2	0	53	0	57.7	59	6	2.0	6.8	43	52.7%	.298

Comparables: James Russell, Jay Ritchie, Nick Wittgren

Is Cimber the solution to the three-true-outcome problem in baseball? A mere 16 percent of the batters he faced walked, homered or struck out, the lowest rate among all hurlers with double-digit frames. Given Cimber's middling career rates, this was probably a small-sample fluke than the new normal. Still, if he keeps it up for much longer Rob Manfred might get some ideas—like, say, forcing every pitcher to rely on mid-80s velocity and a mound-scraping release point. In an alternate reality, there are cardboard cutouts of a mid-delivery Cimber in every bullpen, with signage that instructs "You must release the ball from this low to enter the game." In this reality, he's just trying to stay on the roster for another year.

YEAR	TEAM	LVL	AGE	WHIP	ERA	DRA-	WARP	MPH	FB%	WHF	CSP
2018	SD	MLB	27	1.08	3.17	87	0.6	88.7	75.8%	24.2%	
2018	CLE	MLB	27	1.65	4.05	137	-0.3	89.4	73.5%	12.8%	
2019	CLE	MLB	28	1.32	4.45	107	0.1	87.8	67.8%	20.3%	
2020	CLE	MLB	29	1.32	3.97	100	0.1	87.5	50.8%	22.2%	
2021 FS	MIA	MLB	30	1.25	3.80	91	0.5	88.0	67.1%	20.6%	52.4%
2021 DC	MIA	MLB	30	1.25	3.80	91	0.6	88.0	67.1%	20.6%	52.4%

Adam Cimber, continued

Pitch Shape vs LHH	Pitch Shape vs RHH
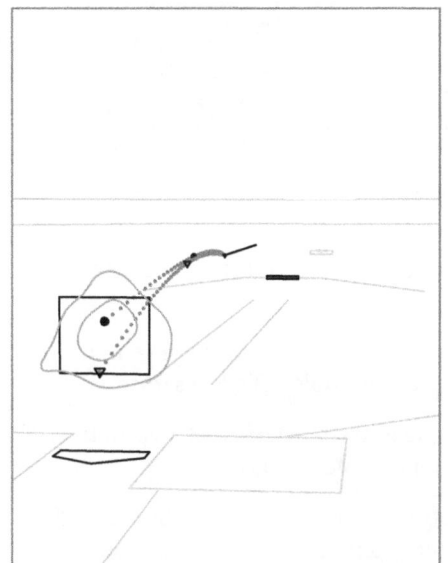	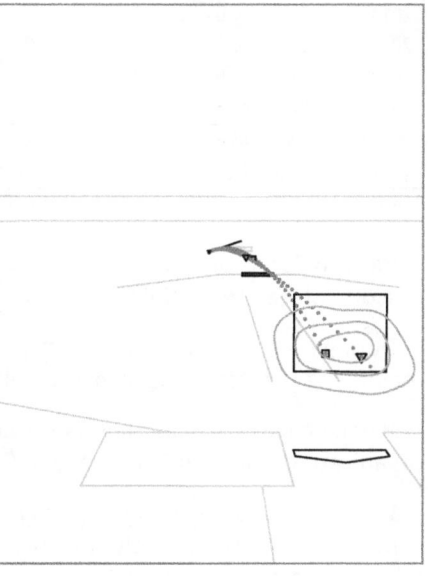

Type	Frequency	Velocity	H Movement	V Movement
● Fastball	28.2%	86.1 [79]	-11.1 [79]	-30.1 [58]
☐ Sinker	22.6%	86 [67]	-12.4 [105]	-39.3 [39]
▽ Slider	49.2%	77 [69]	6.3 [104]	-37.7 [89]

Ross Detwiler   LHP

Born: 03/06/86   Age: 35   Bats: R   Throws: L
Height: 6'5"   Weight: 210   Origin: Round 1, 2007 Draft (#6 overall)

YEAR	TEAM	LVL	AGE	W	L	SV	G	GS	IP	H	HR	BB/9	K/9	K	GB%	BABIP
2018	TAC	AAA	32	2	5	0	16	13	84^2	94	10	2.7	5.5	52	40.9%	.318
2018	SEA	MLB	32	0	1	0	1	0	6	8	1	3.0	3.0	2	52.6%	.389
2019	CHA	AAA	33	1	2	0	8	8	43	44	11	2.3	7.3	35	50.0%	.287
2019	CHW	MLB	33	3	5	0	18	12	69^2	86	20	3.5	5.9	46	50.6%	.304
2020	CHW	MLB	34	1	1	0	16	0	19^2	19	2	2.3	6.9	15	58.3%	.293
2021 FS	MIA	MLB	35	2	3	0	57	0	50	52	7	3.5	6.6	36	49.3%	.293
2021 DC	MIA	MLB	35	2	2	0	53	0	51	54	7	3.5	6.6	37	49.3%	.293

Comparables: Javy Guerra, Homer Bailey, Johnny Cueto

When he's a promising 21-year-old left-hander selected sixth overall out of Missouri State—Potential Hoss Ross.

During his standalone full (mostly), healthy and above-average year in a major league rotation back in 2012 with the Nationals—Big Boss Ross.

When he's pitching in the Atlantic League at the start of 2019, five MLB organizations later—A Rolling Stone Gathers No Moss Ross.

When he's sopping up innings as a mop-up man for the White Sox later that same year, piling up ghastly statistics while pitching through an obvious hip injury—Operating at a Loss Ross.

Living a second (third? fourth?) life as a decently effective reliever, throwing sinkers in 2020—Saucy Rossy

Getting DFA'd at the end of the year anyway—To Live is to Mourn Loss Ross

Catching on with Miami—Live Más Ross

YEAR	TEAM	LVL	AGE	WHIP	ERA	DRA-	WARP	MPH	FB%	WHF	CSP
2018	TAC	AAA	32	1.41	4.89	96	1.0				
2018	SEA	MLB	32	1.67	4.50	144	-0.1	91.0	52.6%	15.0%	
2019	CHA	AAA	33	1.28	3.98	76	1.2				
2019	CHW	MLB	33	1.62	6.59	165	-1.8	93.2	51.5%	16.2%	
2020	CHW	MLB	34	1.22	3.20	86	0.3	93.4	56.9%	27.9%	
2021 FS	MIA	MLB	35	1.45	4.85	110	-0.1	93.2	53.1%	19.5%	50.0%
2021 DC	MIA	MLB	35	1.45	4.85	110	0.0	93.2	53.1%	19.5%	50.0%

Ross Detwiler, continued

Pitch Shape vs LHH	Pitch Shape vs RHH
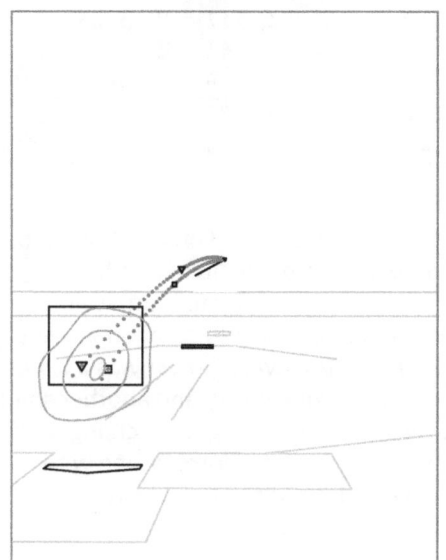	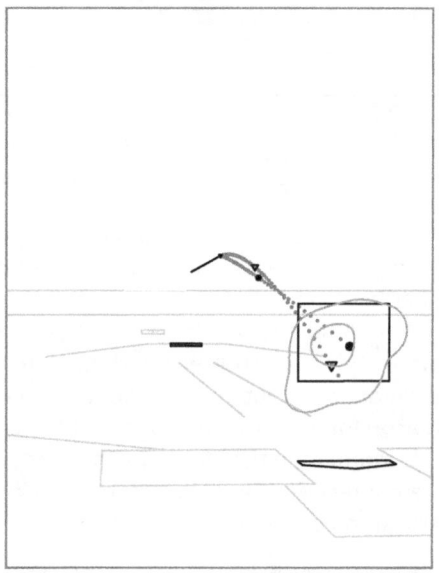

Type	Frequency	Velocity	H Movement	V Movement
● Fastball	27.0%	92.1 [98]	9.9 [85]	-14.4 [102]
☐ Sinker	29.2%	91.2 [94]	14.7 [88]	-20.8 [99]
▲ Changeup	9.2%	85.4 [101]	10.6 [106]	-26.2 [103]
▽ Slider	30.2%	83.4 [97]	-1.3 [85]	-35.5 [95]
◇ Curveball	3.2%	78.6 [100]	-2.2 [78]	-43.6 [111]

Miami Marlins 2021

Dylan Floro   RHP
Born: 12/27/90   Age: 30   Bats: L   Throws: R
Height: 6'2"   Weight: 203   Origin: Round 13, 2012 Draft (#422 overall)

YEAR	TEAM	LVL	AGE	W	L	SV	G	GS	IP	H	HR	BB/9	K/9	K	GB%	BABIP
2018	LAD	MLB	27	3	1	0	29	0	27²	18	1	3.6	10.1	31	52.2%	.254
2018	CIN	MLB	27	3	2	0	25	0	36¹	39	2	3.0	6.7	27	55.8%	.319
2019	LAD	MLB	28	5	3	0	50	0	46²	46	4	2.7	8.1	42	48.3%	.307
2020	LAD	MLB	29	3	0	0	25	0	24¹	23	1	1.5	7.0	19	57.3%	.297
2021 FS	MIA	MLB	30	2	2	3	57	0	50	49	5	2.4	7.5	41	52.7%	.296
2021 DC	MIA	MLB	30	1	1	3	38	0	57.7	56	6	2.4	7.5	48	52.7%	.296

Comparables: Hansel Robles, Tyler Duffey, Mike Morin

The three-batter-minimum rule inspired Floro to work hard on his changeup during the offseason, and in 2020, he became a three-pitch pitcher with two offerings dominating against each type of hitter: sinker-slider to righties and sinker-changeup to lefties. With better feel, he trusted the grip on his changeup more, didn't overthrow it and threw more strikes. The overall effect was a lower strikeout rate, but an exceptionally low opponent exit velocity and another solid season for an above-average middle reliever. Ironically, though, the changeup's real moment in the spotlight came against a righty—when Floro, tasked with stemming the tide in Game 6 of the World Series, retired red-hot Randy Arozarena on three straight cambios.

YEAR	TEAM	LVL	AGE	WHIP	ERA	DRA-	WARP	MPH	FB%	WHF	CSP
2018	LAD	MLB	27	1.05	1.63	70	0.6	95.4	64.8%	31.5%	
2018	CIN	MLB	27	1.40	2.72	117	-0.1	94.9	62.4%	20.9%	
2019	LAD	MLB	28	1.29	4.24	93	0.4	95.4	67.5%	26.3%	
2020	LAD	MLB	29	1.11	2.59	83	0.4	95.0	46.9%	23.3%	
2021 FS	MIA	MLB	30	1.24	3.56	86	0.6	95.2	59.9%	25.1%	48.1%
2021 DC	MIA	MLB	30	1.24	3.56	86	0.7	95.2	59.9%	25.1%	48.1%

Dylan Floro, continued

Pitch Shape vs LHH   **Pitch Shape vs RHH**

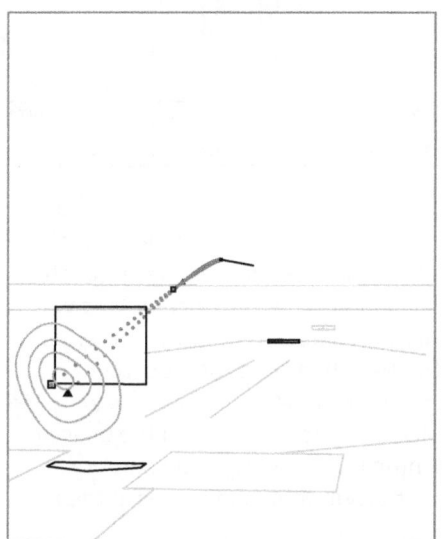 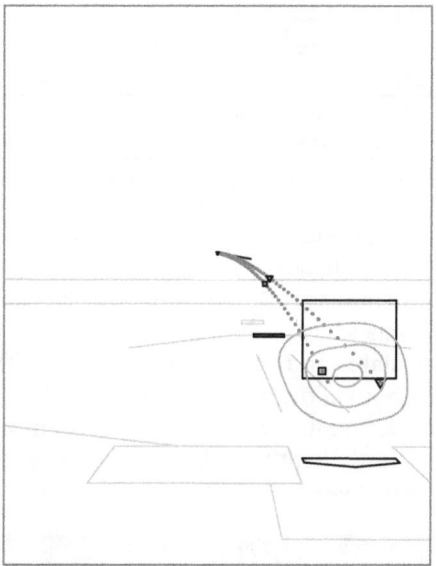

Type	Frequency	Velocity	H Movement	V Movement
☐ Sinker	45.6%	93.4 [105]	-14.3 [91]	-19.2 [104]
▲ Changeup	21.3%	86.2 [104]	-14 [88]	-29.6 [94]
▽ Slider	31.2%	88 [118]	0.5 [82]	-25.2 [125]

Yimi García   RHP

Born: 08/18/90   Age: 30   Bats: R   Throws: R
Height: 6'2"   Weight: 228   Origin: International Free Agent, 2009

YEAR	TEAM	LVL	AGE	W	L	SV	G	GS	IP	H	HR	BB/9	K/9	K	GB%	BABIP
2018	OKC	AAA	27	1	0	1	14	0	14²	16	2	0.0	8.6	14	37.8%	.341
2018	LAD	MLB	27	1	2	0	25	0	22¹	29	7	1.6	7.7	19	35.5%	.319
2019	LAD	MLB	28	1	4	0	64	0	62¹	40	15	2.0	9.5	66	29.2%	.172
2020	MIA	MLB	29	3	0	1	14	0	15	9	0	3.0	11.4	19	47.2%	.250
2021 FS	MIA	MLB	30	2	2	8	57	0	50	42	8	2.4	9.7	53	34.3%	.274
2021 DC	MIA	MLB	30	3	2	8	59	0	57.7	49	9	2.4	9.7	62	34.3%	.274

Comparables: Nick Wittgren, Shawn Armstrong, Emilio Pagán

The Dodgers non-tendered García last winter after a frustratingly homer-prone run. Miami quickly pounced with a major-league contract, reuniting him with manager Don Mattingly, whose last season in Los Angeles coincided with García's best. Mattingly used García as a high-leverage fireman when he was available and García rewarded him with the best 15 innings of his career, without allowing a single homer. There's some reason to believe there were real adjustments buried in the small-sample size here; he's decreased the usage of his fastball rather substantially since returning from Tommy John surgery several years ago, and he induced a lot more grounders than he has in the past.

YEAR	TEAM	LVL	AGE	WHIP	ERA	DRA-	WARP	MPH	FB%	WHF	CSP
2018	OKC	AAA	27	1.09	4.30	49	0.5				
2018	LAD	MLB	27	1.48	5.64	138	-0.3	96.6	56.4%	21.9%	
2019	LAD	MLB	28	0.87	3.61	88	0.7	96.3	46.0%	26.7%	
2020	MIA	MLB	29	0.93	0.60	75	0.3	96.2	49.4%	29.2%	
2021 FS	MIA	MLB	30	1.13	3.47	85	0.7	96.3	48.0%	26.7%	48.4%
2021 DC	MIA	MLB	30	1.13	3.47	85	0.8	96.3	48.0%	26.7%	48.4%

Yimi García, continued

Pitch Shape vs LHH	Pitch Shape vs RHH
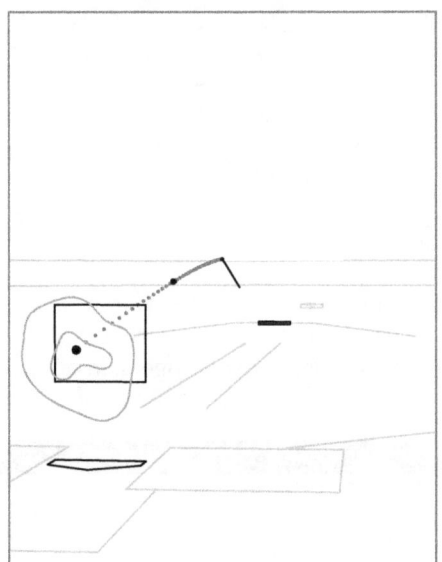	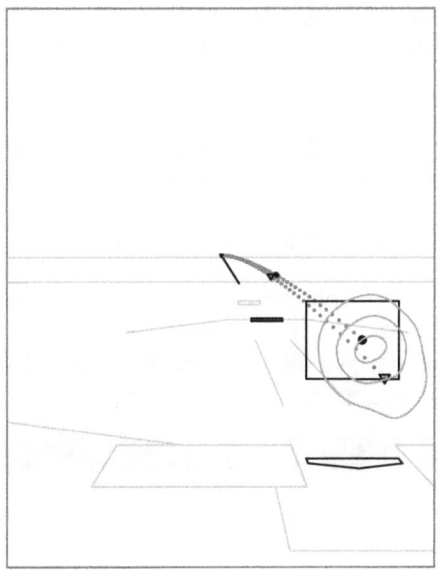

Type	Frequency	Velocity	H Movement	V Movement
● Fastball	49.4%	94.5 [106]	-6 [103]	-16.2 [97]
▲ Changeup	10.4%	87.9 [111]	-15.5 [80]	-30.4 [92]
▽ Slider	29.9%	87.8 [117]	4.5 [97]	-28.5 [115]
◇ Curveball	10.4%	82.2 [114]	10.4 [111]	-39.2 [121]

Miami Marlins 2021

Elieser Hernandez RHP

Born: 05/03/95   Age: 26   Bats: R   Throws: R
Height: 6'0"   Weight: 214   Origin: International Free Agent, 2011

YEAR	TEAM	LVL	AGE	W	L	SV	G	GS	IP	H	HR	BB/9	K/9	K	GB%	BABIP
2018	JUP	HI-A	23	0	1	0	2	2	6	9	2	6.0	7.5	5	68.2%	.350
2018	JAX	AA	23	0	0	0	2	2	9	7	3	4.0	10.0	10	22.7%	.211
2018	MIA	MLB	23	2	7	0	32	6	65^2	68	11	3.7	6.2	45	27.6%	.291
2019	NO	AAA	24	3	1	0	9	9	48	35	0	2.6	12.9	69	32.4%	.315
2019	MIA	MLB	24	3	5	0	21	15	82^1	76	20	2.8	9.3	85	33.5%	.267
2020	MIA	MLB	25	1	0	0	6	6	25^2	21	5	1.8	11.9	34	33.8%	.267
2021 FS	MIA	MLB	26	9	8	0	26	26	150	128	24	3.1	10.1	168	33.5%	.280
2021 DC	MIA	MLB	26	9	7	0	25	25	137.3	117	22	3.1	10.1	154	33.5%	.280

Comparables: Anthony Bass, Alex Reyes, Antonio Senzatela

Miami plucked Hernandez out of the lower levels of Houston's minors via the Rule 5 draft back in 2018. Two years later he looks to be a viable back-end starter with a fastball-slider repertoire who'll give up his fair share of dingers. In other words, a developmental win.

YEAR	TEAM	LVL	AGE	WHIP	ERA	DRA-	WARP	MPH	FB%	WHF	CSP
2018	JUP	HI-A	23	2.17	6.00	92	0.1				
2018	JAX	AA	23	1.22	4.00	89	0.1				
2018	MIA	MLB	23	1.45	5.21	134	-0.7	92.7	62.2%	21.3%	
2019	NO	AAA	24	1.02	1.12	29	2.4				
2019	MIA	MLB	24	1.24	5.03	98	0.9	92.9	55.3%	25.3%	
2020	MIA	MLB	25	1.01	3.16	83	0.5	93.4	58.9%	29.2%	
2021 FS	MIA	MLB	26	1.20	3.78	91	2.2	93.0	57.6%	25.4%	51.0%
2021 DC	MIA	MLB	26	1.20	3.78	91	1.9	93.0	57.6%	25.4%	51.0%

Elieser Hernandez, continued

Pitch Shape vs LHH

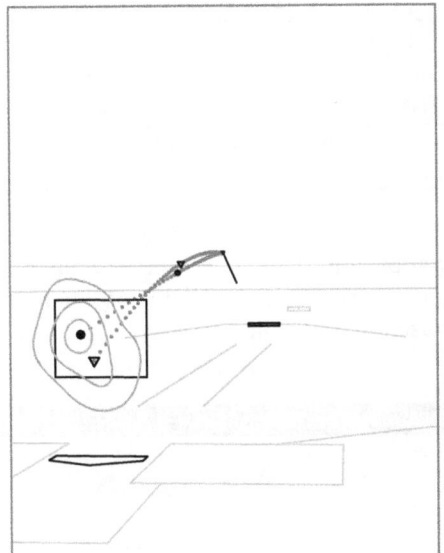

Pitch Shape vs RHH

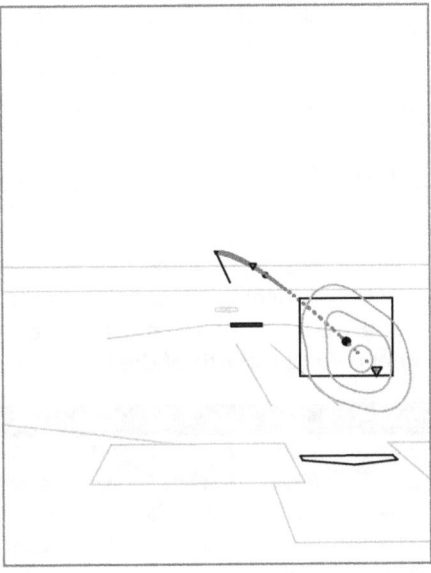

Type	Frequency	Velocity	H Movement	V Movement
● Fastball	58.9%	91.5 [96]	-6.4 [101]	-13.4 [105]
▲ Changeup	6.0%	83.8 [95]	-10.8 [105]	-26.4 [103]
▽ Slider	35.1%	79.2 [79]	10.7 [121]	-29.6 [112]

Miami Marlins 2021

James Hoyt   RHP
Born: 09/30/86   Age: 34   Bats: R   Throws: R
Height: 6'6"   Weight: 230   Origin: Undrafted Free Agent, 2013

YEAR	TEAM	LVL	AGE	W	L	SV	G	GS	IP	H	HR	BB/9	K/9	K	GB%	BABIP
2018	FRE	AAA	31	0	3	5	25	0	28	19	2	2.6	10.6	33	50.0%	.262
2018	HOU	MLB	31	0	0	0	1	0	0^1	1	0	27.0	0.0	0	100.0%	.500
2019	COL	AAA	32	2	0	4	40	2	42	46	3	4.3	10.3	48	52.5%	.374
2019	CLE	MLB	32	0	0	0	8	0	8^1	6	2	2.2	10.8	10	45.0%	.222
2020	MIA	MLB	33	2	0	0	24	0	14^2	9	1	4.9	12.3	20	45.5%	.250
2021 FS	MIA	MLB	34	2	2	0	57	0	50	43	6	3.8	10.3	57	45.2%	.293
2021 DC	MIA	MLB	34	2	2	0	41	0	51	44	6	3.8	10.3	58	45.2%	.293

Comparables: Oliver Drake, Luis García, Chris Hatcher

Formerly a bog-standard 95-and-a-slider up-and-down type who now has a hard time touching 90 mph, Hoyt emerged as a surprisingly reliable option in Miami's 'pen—after his emergency purchase out of DFA limbo—by spamming his slider over two-thirds of the time.

YEAR	TEAM	LVL	AGE	WHIP	ERA	DRA-	WARP	MPH	FB%	WHF	CSP
2018	FRE	AAA	31	0.96	2.25	59	0.8				
2018	HOU	MLB	31	6.00	0.00	46	0.0	94.8	66.7%	25.0%	
2019	COL	AAA	32	1.57	3.43	103	0.5				
2019	CLE	MLB	32	0.96	2.16	105	0.0	95.2	42.3%	40.0%	
2020	MIA	MLB	33	1.16	1.23	81	0.3	90.8	30.6%	35.3%	
2021 FS	MIA	MLB	34	1.29	3.74	88	0.6	92.0	34.0%	36.3%	42.1%
2021 DC	MIA	MLB	34	1.29	3.74	88	0.6	92.0	34.0%	36.3%	42.1%

James Hoyt, continued

Pitch Shape vs LHH

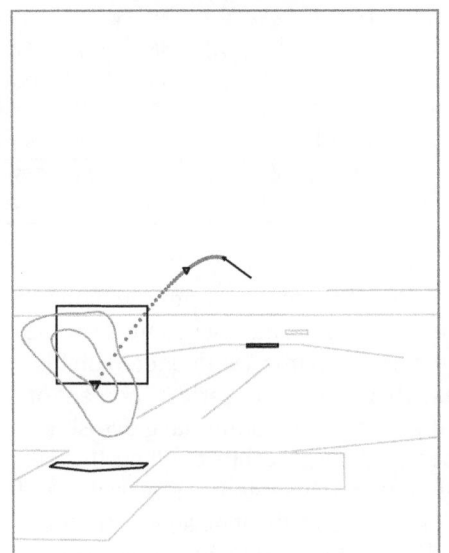

Pitch Shape vs RHH

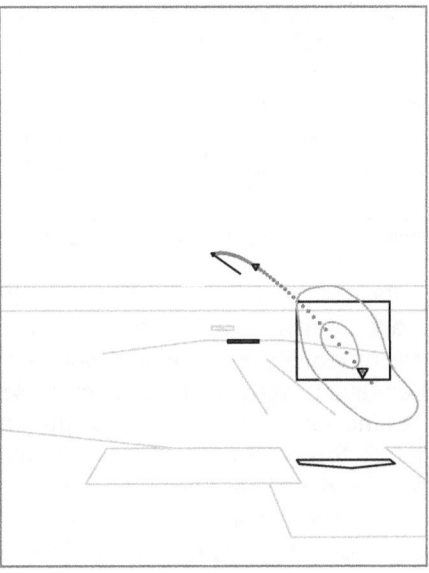

Type	Frequency	Velocity	H Movement	V Movement
● Fastball	17.7%	88.1 [86]	-9.2 [88]	-17 [95]
☐ Sinker	12.4%	89.3 [84]	-15 [86]	-21.7 [96]
▽ Slider	65.9%	80.7 [85]	2.1 [88]	-36.5 [92]

Miami Marlins 2021

Pablo López   RHP

Born: 03/07/96   Age: 25   Bats: L   Throws: R
Height: 6'4"   Weight: 225   Origin: International Free Agent, 2012

YEAR	TEAM	LVL	AGE	W	L	SV	G	GS	IP	H	HR	BB/9	K/9	K	GB%	BABIP
2018	JAX	AA	22	1	2	0	8	8	43^2	30	3	1.6	10.5	51	41.6%	.248
2018	NO	AAA	22	1	1	0	4	4	18^2	16	3	1.9	7.2	15	44.8%	.241
2018	MIA	MLB	22	2	4	0	10	10	58^2	56	8	2.8	7.1	46	49.2%	.282
2019	NO	AAA	23	0	0	0	2	2	9^1	10	0	2.9	9.6	10	61.5%	.385
2019	MIA	MLB	23	5	8	0	21	21	111^1	111	15	2.2	7.7	95	47.3%	.303
2020	MIA	MLB	24	6	4	0	11	11	57^1	50	4	2.8	9.3	59	52.8%	.293
2021 FS	MIA	MLB	25	9	8	0	26	26	150	144	18	2.8	8.5	141	49.1%	.299
2021 DC	MIA	MLB	25	9	7	0	25	25	137.3	132	17	2.8	8.5	129	49.1%	.299

Comparables: Joe Ross, Luke Weaver, Lance McCullers Jr.

One of the catalysts for Miami's sudden playoff surge was López pitching like an ace. Long a command-and-control specialist, López has picked up a couple ticks of velocity in the majors while altering his pitch mix. He ratcheted up his changeup usage in 2020, throwing his best offspeed pitch nearly 30 percent of the time, and developed a new cutter that gave him an additional glove-side look on top of his curveball. He pitched at a Cy Young level through his first six starts, and while he wasn't able to keep it up through September by traditional metrics, his seasonal DRA was still creeping towards elite. If he keeps striking batters out and suppressing hard contact like he did in 2020, he's only a couple hundred innings away from being talked about as one of the best young pitchers in the game, even though he isn't the best young pitcher on the Marlins.

YEAR	TEAM	LVL	AGE	WHIP	ERA	DRA-	WARP	MPH	FB%	WHF	CSP
2018	JAX	AA	22	0.87	0.62	76	0.9				
2018	NO	AAA	22	1.07	3.38	87	0.3				
2018	MIA	MLB	22	1.26	4.14	102	0.5	94.7	60.4%	24.3%	
2019	NO	AAA	23	1.39	1.93	92	0.2				
2019	MIA	MLB	23	1.24	5.09	85	1.9	95.6	58.7%	23.7%	
2020	MIA	MLB	24	1.19	3.61	72	1.4	95.4	63.1%	26.5%	
2021 FS	MIA	MLB	25	1.27	3.87	92	2.1	95.4	60.6%	24.8%	48.1%
2021 DC	MIA	MLB	25	1.27	3.87	92	2.0	95.4	60.6%	24.8%	48.1%

Pablo López, continued

Pitch Shape vs LHH	Pitch Shape vs RHH
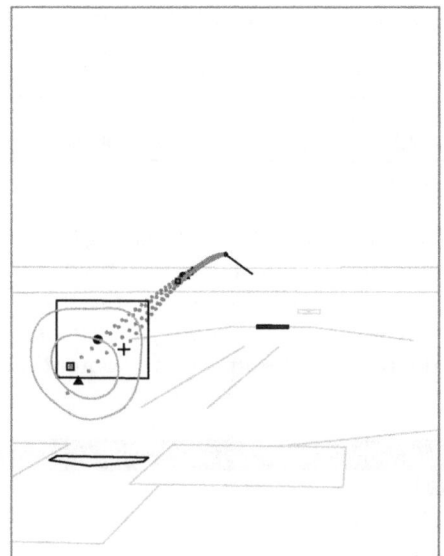	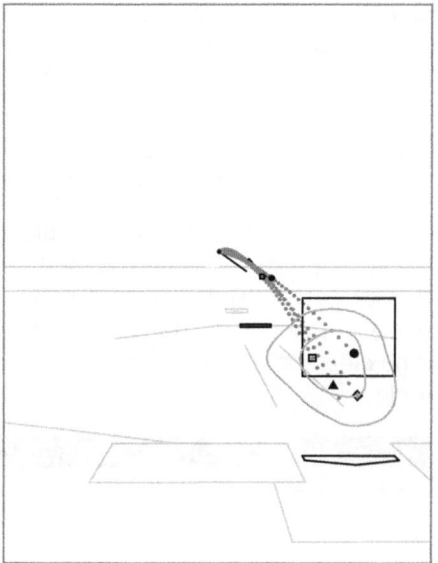

Type	Frequency	Velocity	H Movement	V Movement
● Fastball	32.1%	94.1 [105]	-5.8 [105]	-15.9 [98]
☐ Sinker	22.7%	93.6 [106]	-14 [93]	-21.8 [96]
+ Cutter	8.3%	90.8 [115]	-0.3 [85]	-22.4 [107]
▲ Changeup	29.9%	87.4 [109]	-14.9 [83]	-29.6 [94]
◇ Curveball	7.0%	78.9 [101]	13.1 [122]	-46.3 [105]

Miami Marlins 2021

Nick Neidert RHP
Born: 11/20/96   Age: 24   Bats: R   Throws: R
Height: 6'1"   Weight: 202   Origin: Round 2, 2015 Draft (#60 overall)

YEAR	TEAM	LVL	AGE	W	L	SV	G	GS	IP	H	HR	BB/9	K/9	K	GB%	BABIP
2018	JAX	AA	21	12	7	0	26	26	152.2	142	17	1.8	9.1	154	45.0%	.311
2019	JUP	HI-A	22	0	1	0	2	2	9.1	10	1	3.9	5.8	6	29.0%	.300
2019	NO	AAA	22	3	4	0	9	9	41	45	4	4.8	8.1	37	23.8%	.339
2020	MIA	MLB	23	0	0	0	4	0	8.1	10	1	2.2	4.3	4	60.7%	.333
2021 FS	MIA	MLB	24	2	3	0	57	0	50	52	8	3.3	7.2	40	39.9%	.296
2021 DC	MIA	MLB	24	6	5	0	42	9	77.3	81	12	3.3	7.2	61	39.9%	.296

Comparables: Beau Burrows, Aaron Sanchez, Archie Bradley

A low-90s fastball. A changeup-first offspeed repertoire. Two breaking balls, technically distinguishable but neither distinguished. All of this plus strike-throwing ability and some funk in the delivery. It's a Kyle Hendricks starter kit, right? Kyle Hendricks starter kits are never Kyle Hendricks though, and Neidert is no different. It all adds up to a back of the rotation starter, with the potential for less.

YEAR	TEAM	LVL	AGE	WHIP	ERA	DRA-	WARP	MPH	FB%	WHF	CSP
2018	JAX	AA	21	1.13	3.24	80	2.8				
2019	JUP	HI-A	22	1.50	4.82	110	0.0				
2019	NO	AAA	22	1.63	5.05	117	0.4				
2020	MIA	MLB	23	1.44	5.40	94	0.1	93.2	60.3%	12.9%	
2021 FS	MIA	MLB	24	1.42	4.86	111	-0.1	93.2	60.3%	12.9%	52.4%
2021 DC	MIA	MLB	24	1.42	4.86	111	-0.1	93.2	60.3%	12.9%	52.4%

Nick Neidert, continued

Pitch Shape vs LHH	Pitch Shape vs RHH
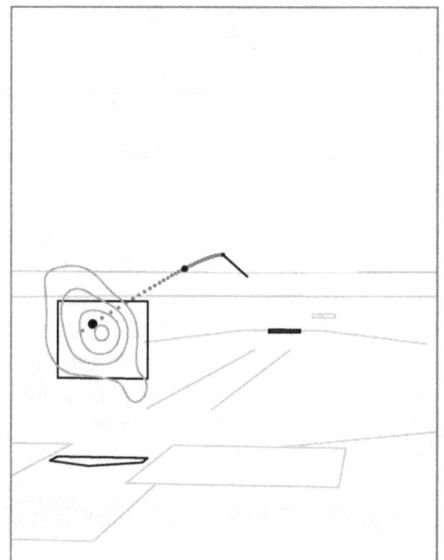	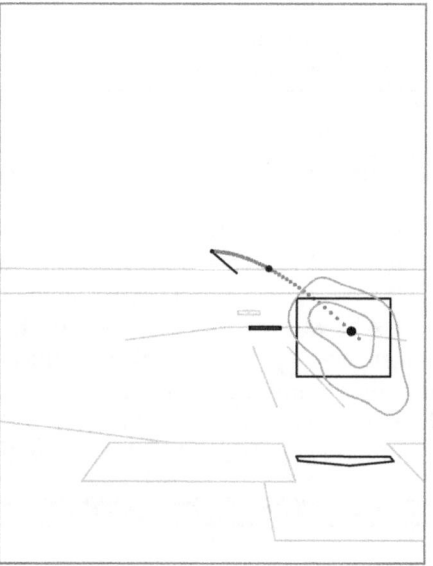

Type	Frequency	Velocity	H Movement	V Movement
● Fastball	59.8%	91.7 [97]	-12.6 [72]	-16.9 [95]
▲ Changeup	18.2%	84.2 [96]	-14.4 [86]	-27.9 [99]
▽ Slider	13.6%	85.5 [107]	0.6 [83]	-26.5 [121]
◇ Curveball	7.6%	74.3 [83]	9.7 [109]	-55.4 [84]

Trevor Rogers LHP

Born: 11/13/97   Age: 23   Bats: L   Throws: L
Height: 6'5"   Weight: 217   Origin: Round 1, 2017 Draft (#13 overall)

YEAR	TEAM	LVL	AGE	W	L	SV	G	GS	IP	H	HR	BB/9	K/9	K	GB%	BABIP
2018	GBO	LO-A	20	2	7	0	17	17	72²	86	4	3.3	10.5	85	46.7%	.398
2019	JUP	HI-A	21	5	8	0	18	18	110¹	97	7	2.0	10.0	122	40.8%	.307
2019	JAX	AA	21	1	2	0	5	5	26	25	3	3.1	9.7	28	28.8%	.319
2020	MIA	MLB	22	1	2	0	7	7	28	32	5	4.2	12.5	39	46.1%	.380
2021 FS	MIA	MLB	23	9	8	0	26	26	150	143	22	3.3	9.3	155	40.4%	.300
2021 DC	MIA	MLB	23	4	5	0	21	17	71	68	10	3.3	9.3	73	40.4%	.300

Comparables: Kris Bubic, Brock Burke, Patrick Sandoval

Pay attention to the DRA on this one. The tall lefty substantially outpitched his ghastly ERA last year, inducing whiffs and managing contact well with both a high-spin fastball and a nasty, sinking changeup. He had one nightmare start where he was torched for nine runs; that hurts more in an abbreviated season. Rogers was a year ahead of schedule reaching the majors with very limited high-minors experience and he was ready for the assignment. He's already come very far over the past two seasons, and further development of his slider and command could vault him further up the major-league rotation.

YEAR	TEAM	LVL	AGE	WHIP	ERA	DRA-	WARP	MPH	FB%	WHF	CSP
2018	GBO	LO-A	20	1.56	5.82	94	0.6				
2019	JUP	HI-A	21	1.10	2.53	80	1.5				
2019	JAX	AA	21	1.31	4.50	102	0.0				
2020	MIA	MLB	22	1.61	6.11	80	0.6	95.8	60.0%	30.1%	
2021 FS	MIA	MLB	23	1.32	4.19	97	1.7	95.8	60.0%	30.1%	47.2%
2021 DC	MIA	MLB	23	1.32	4.19	97	0.8	95.8	60.0%	30.1%	47.2%

Trevor Rogers, continued

Pitch Shape vs LHH	Pitch Shape vs RHH
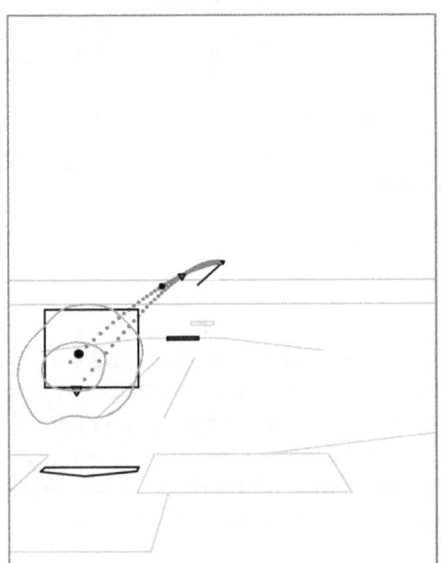	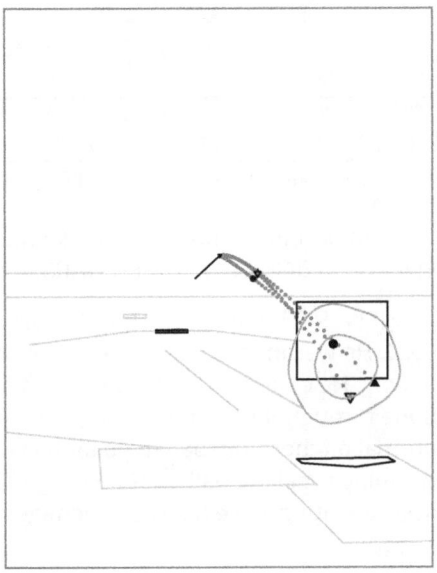

Type	Frequency	Velocity	H Movement	V Movement
● Fastball	60.0%	93.7 [104]	12.4 [73]	-15.1 [100]
▲ Changeup	18.7%	84.5 [97]	13.3 [92]	-34 [82]
▽ Slider	21.3%	81.2 [88]	-1.5 [86]	-34.9 [97]

Marlins Player Analysis - 69

Sixto Sánchez RHP

Born: 07/29/98 Age: 22 Bats: R Throws: R
Height: 6'0" Weight: 234 Origin: International Free Agent, 2015

YEAR	TEAM	LVL	AGE	W	L	SV	G	GS	IP	H	HR	BB/9	K/9	K	GB%	BABIP
2018	CLR	HI-A	19	4	3	0	8	8	46²	39	1	2.1	8.7	45	51.5%	.295
2019	JUP	HI-A	20	0	2	0	2	2	11	14	1	1.6	4.9	6	60.5%	.351
2019	JAX	AA	20	8	4	0	18	18	103	87	5	1.7	8.5	97	47.3%	.288
2020	MIA	MLB	21	3	2	0	7	7	39	36	3	2.5	7.6	33	58.0%	.303
2021 FS	MIA	MLB	22	10	8	0	26	26	150	143	17	2.8	8.1	135	50.2%	.294
2021 DC	MIA	MLB	22	9	7	0	25	25	134.7	128	16	2.8	8.1	121	50.2%	.294

Comparables: Brett Anderson, David Holmberg, Jack Flaherty

An answer in the form of a question. The Final Jeopardy category is EMERGING BASEBALL SUPERSTARS.

ANSWER: This short and stout Miami hurler burst on the national scene in 2020. He was immediately one of the hardest-throwing starting pitchers in the majors. He continued to throw a veritable potpourri of offspeed pitches, as he'd done throughout his minor-league career. His changeup has the speed of a normal pitcher's fastball to go along with filthy movement. He rips off visually stunning breaking balls. His command is present most of the time. He's been an ace-in-waiting since he was a teenager in the Phillies system. He's almost there already.

QUESTION: Who is Sixto Sánchez, Alex?

YEAR	TEAM	LVL	AGE	WHIP	ERA	DRA-	WARP	MPH	FB%	WHF	CSP
2018	CLR	HI-A	19	1.07	2.51	76	0.9				
2019	JUP	HI-A	20	1.45	4.91	117	-0.1				
2019	JAX	AA	20	1.03	2.53	83	1.1				
2020	MIA	MLB	21	1.21	3.46	79	0.8	100.1	47.0%	24.9%	
2021 FS	MIA	MLB	22	1.27	3.73	89	2.4	100.1	47.0%	24.9%	50.1%
2021 DC	MIA	MLB	22	1.27	3.73	89	2.1	100.1	47.0%	24.9%	50.1%

Sixto Sánchez, continued

Pitch Shape vs LHH

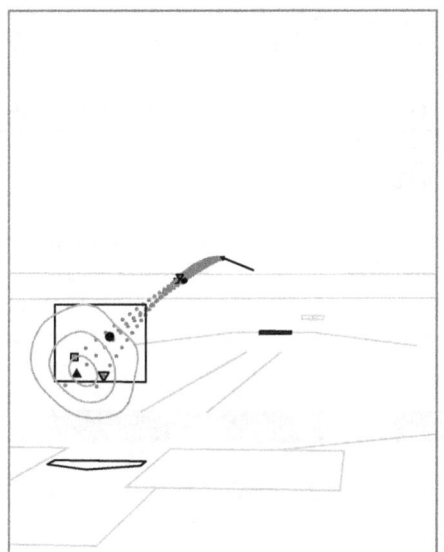

Pitch Shape vs RHH

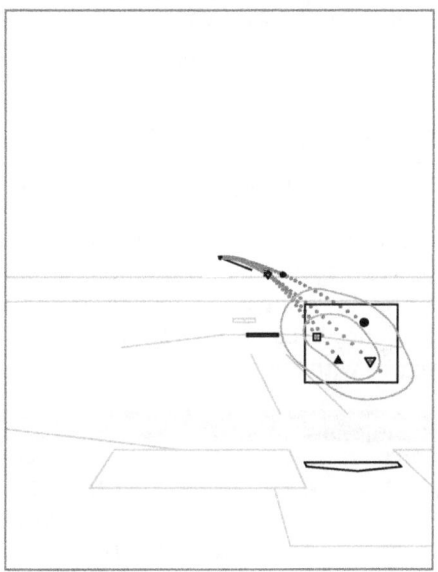

Type	Frequency	Velocity	H Movement	V Movement
● Fastball	23.8%	98.8 [120]	-9.2 [88]	-13.3 [105]
□ Sinker	22.9%	96.9 [123]	-15.5 [82]	-21.8 [96]
▲ Changeup	27.2%	89.3 [116]	-15.2 [81]	-27.7 [99]
▽ Slider	25.4%	88.2 [119]	5.1 [99]	-29.1 [114]

Miami Marlins 2021

Josh A. Smith   RHP
Born: 08/07/87   Age: 33   Bats: R   Throws: R
Height: 6'2"   Weight: 210   Origin: Round 21, 2010 Draft (#637 overall)

YEAR	TEAM	LVL	AGE	W	L	SV	G	GS	IP	H	HR	BB/9	K/9	K	GB%	BABIP
2018	TAC	AAA	30	0	2	0	4	1	10^{1}	17	3	2.6	12.2	14	27.0%	.412
2018	WOR	AAA	30	5	6	1	18	10	74	75	5	1.9	9.2	76	35.2%	.333
2019	WOR	AAA	31	5	3	0	13	12	67^{1}	82	9	2.7	9.4	70	37.9%	.376
2019	BOS	MLB	31	0	3	1	18	2	31	36	10	2.3	8.4	29	34.3%	.292
2020	MIA	MLB	32	1	1	1	16	1	26^{1}	33	3	3.8	6.2	18	42.9%	.345
2021 FS	MIA	MLB	33	2	3	0	57	0	50	50	8	3.0	7.7	42	39.1%	.290

Comparables: Odrisamer Despaigne, Trevor Cahill, Chris Rusin

On June 28, 2018, Pawtucket lefty reliever Josh A. Smith had a three-inning courtesy save in a blowout behind righty starting pitcher Josh D. Smith's six scoreless innings. The Joshes Smith went their separate ways after the season, until they became 2020 Marlins. Their bond will be tested again, as the A version signed with Kiwoom.

YEAR	TEAM	LVL	AGE	WHIP	ERA	DRA-	WARP	MPH	FB%	WHF	CSP
2018	TAC	AAA	30	1.94	6.10	74	0.2				
2018	WOR	AAA	30	1.23	4.14	78	1.3				
2019	WOR	AAA	31	1.51	5.48	121	0.5				
2019	BOS	MLB	31	1.42	5.81	148	-0.6	93.1	38.8%	28.3%	
2020	MIA	MLB	32	1.67	6.84	109	0.1	91.8	35.2%	22.5%	
2021 FS	MIA	MLB	33	1.35	4.56	106	0.1	92.4	36.9%	25.3%	43.8%

Josh A. Smith, continued

Pitch Shape vs LHH

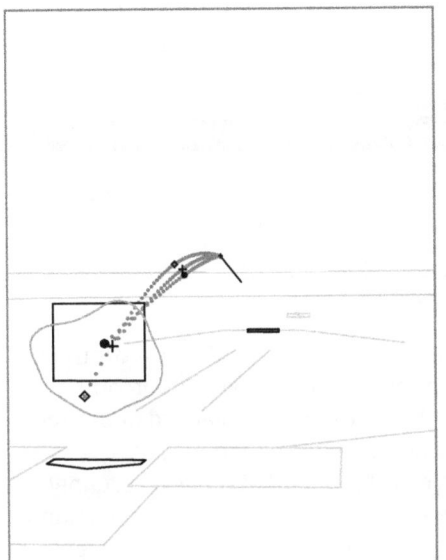

Pitch Shape vs RHH

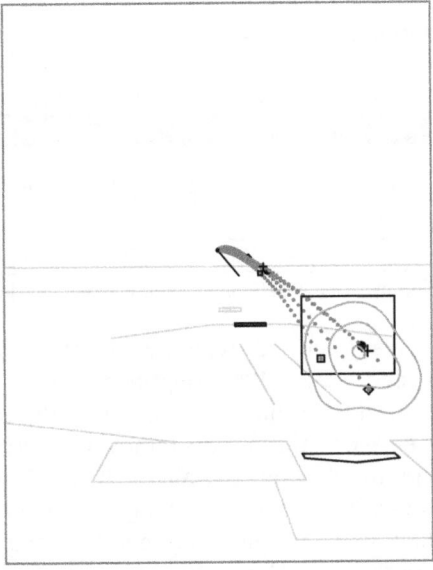

Type	Frequency	Velocity	H Movement	V Movement
● Fastball	19.8%	90.6 [94]	-3.1 [117]	-15.5 [99]
□ Sinker	15.0%	90.3 [89]	-12.6 [103]	-19.7 [103]
+ Cutter	27.2%	86.8 [91]	4.8 [119]	-25.7 [94]
▽ Slider	6.7%	86 [109]	5.7 [102]	-27.7 [118]
◇ Curveball	27.6%	77.8 [97]	14.8 [129]	-47.6 [102]

PLAYER COMMENTS WITHOUT GRAPHS

Eddy Alvarez SS
Born: 01/30/90   Age: 31   Bats: S   Throws: R
Height: 5'9"   Weight: 185   Origin: Undrafted Free Agent, 2014

YEAR	TEAM	LVL	AGE	PA	R	2B	3B	HR	RBI	BB	K	SB	CS	AVG/OBP/SLG
2018	CHA	AAA	28	364	52	26	3	8	37	43	79	5	3	.253/.348/.435
2019	NO	AAA	29	271	45	18	2	12	43	30	53	12	3	.323/.407/.570
2020	MIA	MLB	30	41	6	1	0	0	2	3	16	2	0	.189/.268/.216
2021 FS	MIA	MLB	31	600	58	23	2	14	60	59	174	2	2	.215/.300/.348

Comparables: Tyler Greene, Danny Klassen, Josh Rutledge

Way back in 2014, Eddy the Jet won an Olympic silver medal in short track speed skating. What happened next might be an even unlikelier outcome—he retired from the ice and signed with the White Sox as a 24-year-old undrafted free agent, three years removed from his last baseball experience as a community college walk-on. It wasn't an easy road, and at times it certainly looked like Alvarez wasn't going to make it, but six years and a trade to Miami later he joined Jim Thorpe as the second Olympic medalist from a different sport to play Major League Baseball. He promptly collected his first two major-league hits off Jacob deGrom while filling in around the Marlins infield after their COVID outbreak. The poetic ending would've seen him glide away with a regular job as the Marlins rolled to playoff glory; the real ending is that he's an up-and-down utility player who passed through waivers in September. Life is bittersweet.

YEAR	TEAM	LVL	AGE	PA	DRC+	BABIP	BRR	FRAA	WARP
2018	CHA	AAA	28	364	113	.314	1.7	2B(67): 2.3, SS(31): -3.8, 3B(1): 0.3	1.3
2019	NO	AAA	29	271	129	.374	3.6	3B(33): -2.0, SS(19): 0.5, 2B(10): -1.2	2.0
2020	MIA	MLB	30	41	58	.333	1.4	2B(9): -0.7, 3B(3): 0.3, SS(1): 0.2	0.1
2021 FS	MIA	MLB	31	600	80	.291	-0.4	2B 0, SS -1	0.0

JJ Bleday RF
Born: 11/10/97   Age: 23   Bats: L   Throws: L
Height: 6'3"   Weight: 205   Origin: Round 1, 2019 Draft (#4 overall)

YEAR	TEAM	LVL	AGE	PA	R	2B	3B	HR	RBI	BB	K	SB	CS	AVG/OBP/SLG
2019	JUP	HI-A	21	151	13	8	0	3	19	11	29	0	0	.257/.311/.379
2021 FS	MIA	MLB	23	600	51	24	2	12	56	39	168	1	1	.214/.270/.332

Comparables: Lorenzo Cain, Socrates Brito, Rymer Liriano

The first full professional season for a top college hitting prospect like Bleday usually tells us so much. By now, we very well could have seen him emerge into an elite prospect, or even quickly ascend to the majors like Alex Bregman or Andrew Benintendi did. Instead, he played a bunch of simulated games behind closed doors at the alternate site and instructs. There are no stats to analyze and no first-hand reports to ponder, only rumblings that he performed well. It can be inferred from the lack of a call-up that he probably wasn't an absolute wrecking ball, and if there were major warning signs we'd have probably heard about those, too. Where he fits in the space between, well … maybe we'll get that figured out in 2021.

YEAR	TEAM	LVL	AGE	PA	DRC+	BABIP	BRR	FRAA	WARP
2019	JUP	HI-A	21	151	105	.306	-1.1	RF(32): -0.9	0.1
2021 FS	MIA	MLB	23	600	65	.284	-0.6	RF -11	-2.7

Griffin Conine   OF
Born: 07/11/97   Age: 23   Bats: L   Throws: R
Height: 6'1"   Weight: 213   Origin: Round 2, 2018 Draft (#52 overall)

YEAR	TEAM	LVL	AGE	PA	R	2B	3B	HR	RBI	BB	K	SB	CS	AVG/OBP/SLG
2018	BLU	ROK	20	9	1	1	0	0	3	1	2	0	0	.375/.444/.500
2018	VAN	SS	20	230	24	14	2	7	30	19	63	5	0	.238/.309/.427
2019	LAN	LO-A	21	348	59	19	2	22	64	38	125	2	0	.283/.371/.576
2021 FS	MIA	MLB	23	600	46	20	1	11	50	40	244	2	1	.175/.237/.279

Comparables: Jaylin Davis, Zoilo Almonte, Jesús Aguilar

It was always destiny, wasn't it? The son of "Mr. Marlin" Jeff Conine was born in 1997 in South Florida, when his pops manned first base for a Marlins squad about to go on a magical World Series run. Twenty-three summers later, he came home in the Jonathan Villar deal. Like his dad, Griffin is a bat-first corner type; he projects to hit for more power than Jeff did, but also has a long way to go before you can project him to play in the bigs for 17 years. It's got the potential to be a great story if his hit tool can live up to it.

YEAR	TEAM	LVL	AGE	PA	DRC+	BABIP	BRR	FRAA	WARP
2018	BLU	ROK	20	9		.500			
2018	VAN	SS	20	230	93	.304	-1.5	RF(46): 10.1	0.4
2019	LAN	LO-A	21	348	155	.405	2.8	RF(74): 6.2	3.7
2021 FS	MIA	MLB	23	600	42	.286	-0.5	RF 16	-1.7

Miami Marlins 2021

José Devers SS
Born: 12/07/99 Age: 21 Bats: L Throws: R
Height: 6'0" Weight: 174 Origin: International Free Agent, 2016

YEAR	TEAM	LVL	AGE	PA	R	2B	3B	HR	RBI	BB	K	SB	CS	AVG/OBP/SLG
2018	GBO	LO-A	18	362	46	12	4	0	24	15	49	13	6	.273/.313/.332
2019	MRL	ROK	19	46	7	3	1	0	2	4	4	3	1	.275/.370/.400
2019	JUP	HI-A	19	138	13	3	1	0	3	8	20	5	0	.325/.384/.365
2021 FS	MIA	MLB	21	600	48	24	3	6	50	32	143	11	4	.230/.283/.323

Comparables: Ketel Marte, Cole Tucker, Sergio Alcántara

Best remembered for who he isn't—Giancarlo Stanton, for whom he was traded, and his cousin Rafael—Devers is an interesting prospect in his own right. He's smooth with his glove at an up-the-middle position and last we saw him on a minor-league field, he even hit a little bit. That was back in 2019, but Devers did spend the summer at the alternate site, developing in front of the watchful eyes of the Marlins professional staff. Despite only 35 career games in High-A, it's possible Devers is on the fast track, given that the Marlins snuck him on to their taxi squad when they made the playoffs.

YEAR	TEAM	LVL	AGE	PA	DRC+	BABIP	BRR	FRAA	WARP
2018	GBO	LO-A	18	362	92	.318	-2.6	SS(58): 2.2, 2B(15): 0.0	0.2
2019	MRL	ROK	19	46		.306			
2019	JUP	HI-A	19	138	128	.387	-1.8	SS(32): -1.9	0.6
2021 FS	MIA	MLB	21	600	67	.299	0.8	SS -1, 2B 1	-0.7

Isan Díaz 2B
Born: 05/27/96 Age: 25 Bats: L Throws: R
Height: 5'11" Weight: 201 Origin: Round 2, 2014 Draft (#70 overall)

YEAR	TEAM	LVL	AGE	PA	R	2B	3B	HR	RBI	BB	K	SB	CS	AVG/OBP/SLG
2018	JAX	AA	22	355	44	19	1	10	42	53	95	10	3	.245/.364/.418
2018	NO	AAA	22	155	19	4	4	3	14	15	45	4	0	.204/.281/.358
2019	NO	AAA	23	435	89	21	2	26	70	49	96	5	4	.305/.395/.578
2019	MIA	MLB	23	201	17	5	2	5	23	19	59	0	3	.173/.259/.307
2020	MIA	MLB	24	22	3	0	0	0	1	0	7	0	0	.182/.182/.182
2021 FS	MIA	MLB	25	600	71	22	3	22	70	58	195	2	2	.214/.298/.395
2021 DC	MIA	MLB	25	323	38	12	1	12	37	31	105	1	1	.214/.298/.395

Comparables: Ernie Fazio, Jerry Buchek, Garrett Hampson

While quarantined in Philadelphia after 18 of his teammates came down with COVID, Díaz opted out of the 2020 season. Even though he quite understandably opted out in the middle of the league's worst outbreak of 2020, the Marlins placed him on the restricted list without pay or service time, a patently ludicrous bit of "business" that will gain them an extra year of team control down the line. He ultimately opted back into the season around the trade deadline, spurring Miami to deal Jonathan Villar, and promptly suffered a season-ending groin injury upon his return from the alternate site. Through it all, he remains a promising young hitter with major power potential, though a season of lost reps clouds his long-term development.

YEAR	TEAM	LVL	AGE	PA	DRC+	BABIP	BRR	FRAA	WARP
2018	JAX	AA	22	355	121	.325	0.0	2B(82): 2.1	1.4
2018	NO	AAA	22	155	65	.278	0.8	2B(35): -1.6	-0.4
2019	NO	AAA	23	435	132	.349	0.7	2B(99): 0.8	3.1
2019	MIA	MLB	23	201	62	.224	0.1	2B(48): 0.0	-0.3
2020	MIA	MLB	24	22	77	.267	0.0	2B(7): 0.8	0.1
2021 FS	MIA	MLB	25	600	89	.289	-0.2	2B 0	1.0
2021 DC	MIA	MLB	25	323	89	.289	-0.1	2B 0	0.5

Miami Marlins 2021

Lewin Díaz 1B
Born: 11/19/96   Age: 24   Bats: L   Throws: L
Height: 6'4"   Weight: 217   Origin: International Free Agent, 2013

YEAR	TEAM	LVL	AGE	PA	R	2B	3B	HR	RBI	BB	K	SB	CS	AVG/OBP/SLG
2018	FTM	HI-A	21	310	21	11	3	6	35	10	56	1	0	.224/.255/.344
2019	FTM	HI-A	22	234	34	11	1	13	36	14	40	0	0	.290/.333/.533
2019	JAX	AA	22	129	16	6	0	8	14	11	28	0	1	.200/.279/.461
2019	PNS	AA	22	138	12	16	1	6	26	8	23	0	0	.302/.341/.587
2020	MIA	MLB	23	41	2	2	0	0	3	2	12	0	0	.154/.195/.205
2021 FS	MIA	MLB	24	600	67	25	2	23	78	37	166	0	1	.219/.273/.401
2021 DC	MIA	MLB	24	132	14	5	0	5	17	8	36	0	0	.219/.273/.401

Comparables: Kendrys Morales, Russ Canzler, Ben Paulsen

Díaz was a nice get for Sergio Romo at the 2019 trade deadline, having been in the midst of a breakout season in which his power was finally showing up in games. He was brought up a year early out of brief necessity and didn't stick, but it's safe to assume he'll be ready for a longer look next year.

YEAR	TEAM	LVL	AGE	PA	DRC+	BABIP	BRR	FRAA	WARP
2018	FTM	HI-A	21	310	67	.255	-1.8	1B(74): 2.7	-1.3
2019	FTM	HI-A	22	234	157	.297	-1.3	1B(52): 4.9	2.0
2019	JAX	AA	22	129	122	.188	-0.2	1B(30): -2.2	0.5
2019	PNS	AA	22	138	130	.320	-0.6	1B(31): -0.2	0.9
2020	MIA	MLB	23	41	73	.222	-0.1	1B(11): 0.9	0.0
2021 FS	MIA	MLB	24	600	80	.268	-0.7	1B 1	-0.6
2021 DC	MIA	MLB	24	132	80	.268	-0.1	1B 0	-0.1

Jerar Encarnación RF
Born: 10/22/97   Age: 23   Bats: R   Throws: R
Height: 6'5"   Weight: 239   Origin: International Free Agent, 2015

YEAR	TEAM	LVL	AGE	PA	R	2B	3B	HR	RBI	BB	K	SB	CS	AVG/OBP/SLG
2018	BAT	SS	20	190	30	14	2	4	24	4	57	1	1	.284/.305/.448
2018	GBO	LO-A	20	59	3	0	0	0	2	5	23	0	0	.074/.153/.074
2019	CLI	LO-A	21	281	34	16	0	10	43	23	69	3	1	.298/.363/.478
2019	JUP	HI-A	21	272	27	10	1	6	28	17	71	3	2	.253/.298/.372
2021 FS	MIA	MLB	23	600	52	22	2	16	61	34	230	1	1	.203/.253/.339

Comparables: Jorge Oña, Socrates Brito, Rymer Liriano

Encarnacion was a surprise inclusion on Miami's summer camp roster. He's a massive man with light tower power and questionable bat-to-ball ability, so a summer's worth of reps against advanced pitching was certainly better than hitting off a JUGS machine.

YEAR	TEAM	LVL	AGE	PA	DRC+	BABIP	BRR	FRAA	WARP
2018	BAT	SS	20	190	87	.390	-0.3	RF(37): 9.8	0.5
2018	GBO	LO-A	20	59	-3	.129	-0.2	RF(12): 5.7, 1B(1): -0.0	-0.1
2019	CLI	LO-A	21	281	141	.375	-1.6	RF(63): 7.2	2.3
2019	JUP	HI-A	21	272	101	.326	-1.9	RF(31): 5.8, LF(23): -1.1, 1B(3): -0.0	0.8
2021 FS	MIA	MLB	23	600	59	.310	-0.5	RF 14, LF 1	-0.4

Monte Harrison CF
Born: 08/10/95   Age: 25   Bats: R   Throws: R
Height: 6'3"   Weight: 225   Origin: Round 2, 2014 Draft (#50 overall)

YEAR	TEAM	LVL	AGE	PA	R	2B	3B	HR	RBI	BB	K	SB	CS	AVG/OBP/SLG
2018	JAX	AA	22	583	85	20	3	19	48	44	215	28	9	.240/.316/.399
2019	NO	AAA	23	244	41	7	2	9	24	25	73	20	2	.274/.357/.451
2020	MIA	MLB	24	51	8	1	0	1	3	4	26	6	0	.170/.235/.255
2021 FS	MIA	MLB	25	600	62	20	2	14	55	45	256	13	4	.188/.265/.315
2021 DC	MIA	MLB	25	120	12	4	0	2	11	9	51	2	1	.188/.265/.315

Comparables: Dave Krynzel, Jai Miller, Greg Halman

There were a lot of overmatched Marlins prospects pressed into duty in 2020, but Harrison was at the head of the class. He struck out over half the time in his debut season, amplifying severe swing-and-miss issues that have threatened his hit tool ever since he came over from Milwaukee. When he did hit it, he didn't hit it that hard: He averaged 81.7 mph in terms of exit velocity, near the very bottom of the majors. Harrison has tried all kinds of swing changes to increase his ability to make contact, but he hasn't found a bat path that has consistently gotten him to strike the ball hard yet. Unlike some of the other emergency Marlins, Harrison had enough high-minors experience (192 games) that he shouldn't have been quite this overwhelmed by major-league pitching. He needs to find a swing and setup that will actually work, lest he find himself in the same position as outfield-mate Lewis Brinson.

YEAR	TEAM	LVL	AGE	PA	DRC+	BABIP	BRR	FRAA	WARP
2018	JAX	AA	22	583	96	.368	3.6	CF(120): -8.0, RF(14): 0.4	0.1
2019	NO	AAA	23	244	93	.373	3.2	CF(32): 2.6, RF(19): -2.4, LF(3): 0.8	0.9
2020	MIA	MLB	24	51	51	.350	0.1	CF(16): 1.5, RF(13): 0.4	0.0
2021 FS	MIA	MLB	25	600	61	.321	0.9	CF 2, RF 0	-1.1
2021 DC	MIA	MLB	25	120	61	.321	0.2	CF 0, RF 0	-0.3

Sandy León C

Born: 03/13/89   Age: 32   Bats: S   Throws: R
Height: 5'10"   Weight: 235   Origin: International Free Agent, 2007

YEAR	TEAM	LVL	AGE	PA	R	2B	3B	HR	RBI	BB	K	SB	CS	AVG/OBP/SLG
2018	BOS	MLB	29	288	30	12	0	5	22	15	75	1	0	.177/.232/.279
2019	WOR	AAA	30	26	2	0	0	0	0	1	6	0	1	.120/.154/.120
2019	BOS	MLB	30	191	14	3	0	5	19	13	47	0	0	.192/.251/.297
2020	CLE	MLB	31	81	4	1	0	2	4	14	21	0	0	.136/.296/.242
2021 FS	MIA	MLB	32	600	57	22	1	15	60	52	164	1	1	.209/.287/.340

Comparables: Martín Maldonado, Todd Pratt, Bob Geren

Terry Francona is prone to describing León as a future manager. He, along with the rest of Cleveland's catchers, sure hit like skippers in 2020. Cleveland's catchers collectively hit .135/.251/.197, the all-time worst performance of any position relative to the league OPS. There's no doubt

YEAR	TEAM	P. COUNT	FRM RUNS	BLK RUNS	THRW RUNS	TOT RUNS
2018	BOS	11245	11.6	0.1	0.1	11.8
2019	BOS	8122	4.8	-1.0	-0.2	3.6
2020	CLE	3027	1.1	-0.1	0.0	1.0
2021	MIA	16650	6.6	-1.6	-0.2	4.8
2021	MIA	16650	6.6	-0.9	-0.2	5.5

that León's luck on balls in play was rotten. He also had a terribly inconsistent routine, going from Yadi-esque usage with six consecutive starts in mid-August, to dealing with more important matters on the family medical emergency list, then receiving only sporadic appearances in September after Cleveland acquired Hedges. Despite all that, León should take solace in knowing he was Cleveland's best producer behind the plate—and that if and when he's done playing, he'll probably prove Francona's assertion about his future correct.

YEAR	TEAM	LVL	AGE	PA	DRC+	BABIP	BRR	FRAA	WARP
2018	BOS	MLB	29	288	57	.226	-0.7	C(87): 11.7	1.1
2019	WOR	AAA	30	26	30	.158	-0.5	C(7): 0.8	-0.1
2019	BOS	MLB	30	191	65	.231	-0.2	C(65): 2.9, 1B(1): -0.0	0.4
2020	CLE	MLB	31	81	90	.163	-0.4	C(24): 0.7	0.3
2021 FS	MIA	MLB	32	600	72	.272	-0.8	C 5, 1B 0	0.7

Kameron Misner   OF

Born: 01/08/98   Age: 23   Bats: L   Throws: L
Height: 6'4"   Weight: 218   Origin: Round 1, 2019 Draft (#35 overall)

YEAR	TEAM	LVL	AGE	PA	R	2B	3B	HR	RBI	BB	K	SB	CS	AVG/OBP/SLG
2019	MRL	ROK	21	38	2	2	0	0	4	9	7	3	0	.241/.421/.310
2019	CLI	LO-A	21	158	25	7	0	2	20	21	35	8	0	.276/.380/.373
2021 FS	MIA	MLB	23	600	52	22	2	10	53	52	186	9	2	.205/.281/.313

Comparables: Ryan LaMarre, Mitch Haniger, Gary Brown

A 2019 SEC first-rounder would seem to be a lock to show up at the alternate site at some point, but Miami never invited Misner, which can't be a good sign for his development track. He did participate in the fall instructional league, so at least we know he's healthy.

YEAR	TEAM	LVL	AGE	PA	DRC+	BABIP	BRR	FRAA	WARP
2019	MRL	ROK	21	38		.318			
2019	CLI	LO-A	21	158	136	.357	2.2	CF(32): 7.1	2.0
2021 FS	MIA	MLB	23	600	66	.291	0.3	CF 25, RF 0	1.8

Harold Ramirez   CF

Born: 09/06/94   Age: 26   Bats: R   Throws: R
Height: 5'10"   Weight: 232   Origin: International Free Agent, 2011

YEAR	TEAM	LVL	AGE	PA	R	2B	3B	HR	RBI	BB	K	SB	CS	AVG/OBP/SLG
2018	NH	AA	23	505	60	37	0	11	70	27	88	16	2	.320/.365/.471
2019	NO	AAA	24	120	19	12	1	4	14	6	19	1	1	.355/.408/.591
2019	MIA	MLB	24	446	54	20	3	11	50	18	91	2	1	.276/.312/.416
2020	MIA	MLB	25	11	2	0	0	0	1	1	2	0	1	.200/.273/.200
2021 FS	MIA	MLB	26	600	65	27	2	14	69	31	130	2	2	.262/.314/.399
2021 DC	MIA	MLB	26	134	14	6	0	3	15	7	29	0	1	.262/.314/.399

Comparables: Todd Hollandsworth, Alfonso Soriano, Mark Brouhard

The Opening Day right fielder looked poised to play a big role in the outfield; he missed time with COVID and then suffered a season-ending hamstring injury in his first game after recovering.

YEAR	TEAM	LVL	AGE	PA	DRC+	BABIP	BRR	FRAA	WARP
2018	NH	AA	23	505	131	.371	2.5	RF(61): -2.7, LF(18): -0.5	1.7
2019	NO	AAA	24	120	122	.402	-2.3	LF(16): -0.2, RF(8): 0.1	0.4
2019	MIA	MLB	24	446	84	.328	-0.2	LF(61): 4.1, RF(55): -2.5, CF(27): 2.2	0.7
2020	MIA	MLB	25	11	79	.250		RF(2): -0.1, LF(1): 0.0	0.0
2021 FS	MIA	MLB	26	600	95	.320	-0.4	LF 3, RF 0	1.3
2021 DC	MIA	MLB	26	134	95	.320	-0.1	LF 1, RF 0	0.3

Miami Marlins 2021

Jesús Sánchez RF
Born: 10/07/97 Age: 23 Bats: L Throws: R
Height: 6'3" Weight: 222 Origin: International Free Agent, 2014

YEAR	TEAM	LVL	AGE	PA	R	2B	3B	HR	RBI	BB	K	SB	CS	AVG/OBP/SLG
2018	CHA	HI-A	20	378	56	24	2	10	64	15	71	6	3	.301/.331/.462
2018	MTG	AA	20	110	14	8	0	1	11	11	21	1	1	.214/.300/.327
2019	MTG	AA	21	316	32	11	1	8	49	24	65	5	4	.275/.332/.404
2019	NO	AAA	21	78	11	1	0	4	9	9	15	0	0	.246/.338/.446
2019	DUR	AAA	21	71	6	2	1	1	5	6	20	0	0	.206/.282/.317
2020	MIA	MLB	22	29	1	1	0	0	2	4	11	0	0	.040/.172/.080
2021 FS	MIA	MLB	23	600	62	27	4	17	65	41	172	1	1	.235/.291/.392
2021 DC	MIA	MLB	23	157	16	7	1	4	17	10	45	0	0	.235/.291/.392

Comparables: Brandon Moss, Tyler Austin, Jeff Francoeur

The Marlins gave Sánchez a clean shot to win the right field job in late-August. He looked completely overmatched at the plate, losing his starting spot in a week and his roster spot just a few days later, never to return. He has the barrel control and swing to project a plus hit tool and substantial raw power, but it just hasn't clicked yet. It's been years now since we've seen the whole package work together. Hitters hit, and Sánchez hasn't hit anywhere since A-ball.

YEAR	TEAM	LVL	AGE	PA	DRC+	BABIP	BRR	FRAA	WARP
2018	CHA	HI-A	20	378	133	.350	-1.5	RF(78): 1.8, CF(7): -1.4	1.2
2018	MTG	AA	20	110	93	.263	0.7	RF(26): -0.8, CF(1): -0.0	-0.1
2019	MTG	AA	21	316	121	.327	0.1	RF(72): 0.0	1.4
2019	NO	AAA	21	78	73	.250	0.3	CF(8): -1.6, RF(8): 3.6	0.2
2019	DUR	AAA	21	71	52	.279	-0.3	RF(15): 0.7	-0.2
2020	MIA	MLB	22	29	81	.071	0.0	RF(10): 0.4	0.0
2021 FS	MIA	MLB	23	600	84	.310	-0.3	RF 6, CF -2	0.4
2021 DC	MIA	MLB	23	157	84	.310	-0.1	RF 1, CF -1	0.1

Connor Scott OF
Born: 10/08/99   Age: 21   Bats: L   Throws: L
Height: 6'3"   Weight: 187   Origin: Round 1, 2018 Draft (#13 overall)

YEAR	TEAM	LVL	AGE	PA	R	2B	3B	HR	RBI	BB	K	SB	CS	AVG/OBP/SLG
2018	MRL	ROK	18	119	15	1	4	0	8	14	29	8	5	.223/.319/.311
2018	GBO	LO-A	18	89	4	2	0	1	5	10	27	1	3	.211/.295/.276
2019	CLI	LO-A	19	413	56	24	4	4	36	31	91	21	9	.251/.311/.368
2019	JUP	HI-A	19	111	12	4	1	1	5	11	26	2	1	.235/.306/.327
2021 FS	MIA	MLB	21	600	46	22	4	8	49	43	199	10	8	.200/.261/.301

Comparables: Mickey Moniak, Rey Fuentes, Derrick Robinson

Scott is fast and can glove it in center. The bat projection is there, somewhere—you don't get drafted that high without offensive projection—but it hasn't shown up as a pro yet, although he's had challenging assignments thus far.

YEAR	TEAM	LVL	AGE	PA	DRC+	BABIP	BRR	FRAA	WARP
2018	MRL	ROK	18	119		.307			
2018	GBO	LO-A	18	89	58	.300	-1.9	CF(22): -3.0	-0.8
2019	CLI	LO-A	19	413	98	.322	1.6	CF(85): -2.6, LF(1): -0.1	1.1
2019	JUP	HI-A	19	111	85	.301	0.9	CF(24): -1.5	0.1
2021 FS	MIA	MLB	21	600	54	.297	1.3	CF 3, LF 0	-1.2

Jeff Brigham RHP
Born: 02/16/92   Age: 29   Bats: R   Throws: R
Height: 6'0"   Weight: 195   Origin: Round 4, 2014 Draft (#129 overall)

YEAR	TEAM	LVL	AGE	W	L	SV	G	GS	IP	H	HR	BB/9	K/9	K	GB%	BABIP
2018	JAX	AA	26	4	1	0	7	7	38	27	1	2.1	9.7	41	40.9%	.299
2018	NO	AAA	26	5	2	0	9	9	52^1	53	7	2.2	8.3	48	28.1%	.319
2018	MIA	MLB	26	0	4	0	4	4	16^1	16	2	7.2	6.6	12	18.0%	.292
2019	NO	AAA	27	0	1	2	17	0	24	9	0	3.0	11.2	30	40.8%	.184
2019	MIA	MLB	27	3	2	1	32	0	38^1	36	8	3.3	9.2	39	32.7%	.283
2020	MIA	MLB	28	0	0	0	1	0	1	2	0	0.0	0.0	0	0.0%	.400
2021 FS	MIA	MLB	29	2	2	0	57	0	50	45	9	3.4	9.0	50	32.8%	.274
2021 DC	MIA	MLB	29	1	1	0	33	0	32	28	5	3.4	9.0	32	32.8%	.274

Comparables: Alec Mills, Kelvin Marte, Glenn Sparkman

We can all relate to Brigham's 2020, a tale of fleeting hope sandwiched by lengthy disappointments. Sidelined in the preseason by a biceps injury, he would have missed months of action—if there had been any. COVID-19 gave him time to recover and return for a single inning, then ended his season with a positive test.

Miami Marlins 2021

YEAR	TEAM	LVL	AGE	WHIP	ERA	DRA-	WARP	MPH	FB%	WHF	CSP
2018	JAX	AA	26	0.95	1.18	91	0.4				
2018	NO	AAA	26	1.26	3.44	85	0.9				
2018	MIA	MLB	26	1.78	6.06	160	-0.4	94.9	61.1%	19.9%	
2019	NO	AAA	27	0.71	1.50	20	1.2				
2019	MIA	MLB	27	1.30	4.46	97	0.3	98.0	51.5%	25.4%	
2020	MIA	MLB	28	2.00	9.00	112	0.0	95.0	68.2%	0.0%	
2021 FS	MIA	MLB	29	1.28	4.24	99	0.3	97.3	53.9%	23.4%	49.5%
2021 DC	MIA	MLB	29	1.28	4.24	99	0.2	97.3	53.9%	23.4%	49.5%

Edward Cabrera   RHP
Born: 04/13/98   Age: 23   Bats: R   Throws: R
Height: 6'5"   Weight: 217   Origin: International Free Agent, 2015

YEAR	TEAM	LVL	AGE	W	L	SV	G	GS	IP	H	HR	BB/9	K/9	K	GB%	BABIP
2018	GBO	LO-A	20	4	8	0	22	22	100^1	105	11	3.8	8.3	93	43.4%	.329
2019	JUP	HI-A	21	5	3	0	11	11	58	37	1	2.8	11.3	73	47.3%	.281
2019	JAX	AA	21	4	1	0	8	8	38^2	28	6	3.0	10.0	43	48.5%	.242
2021 FS	MIA	MLB	23	2	3	0	57	0	50	47	7	4.0	8.6	47	44.3%	.288
2021 DC	MIA	MLB	23	3	3	0	6	11	47.3	44	7	4.0	8.6	45	44.3%	.288

Comparables: Jonathan Hernández, Gerrit Cole, Frankie Montas

Most top pitching prospects with upper-minors experience debuted in 2020 as compressed schedules forced nearly every team's hand. Despite Miami's pressing pitching needs, Cabrera did not. He suffered from minor arm issues towards the end of summer camp and the Marlins handled his ramp-up very carefully at the alternate site. By the time the playoffs rolled around he was throwing simulated games as part of the taxi squad, and he very well might've shown up if the team had advanced a little further. We're still in on him, even if major question marks remain about whether he's a starter or reliever long-term.

YEAR	TEAM	LVL	AGE	WHIP	ERA	DRA-	WARP	MPH	FB%	WHF	CSP
2018	GBO	LO-A	20	1.47	4.22	139	-1.7				
2019	JUP	HI-A	21	0.95	2.02	62	1.4				
2019	JAX	AA	21	1.06	2.56	70	0.7				
2021 FS	MIA	MLB	23	1.39	4.56	106	0.1				
2021 DC	MIA	MLB	23	1.39	4.56	106	0.3				

Dax Fulton LHP
Born: 10/16/01   Age: 19   Bats: L   Throws: L
Height: 6'6"   Weight: 230   Origin: Round 2, 2020 Draft (#40 overall)

One of the best prep pitchers in the 2020 Draft, Fulton was still available to the Marlins at the 40th pick because of September 2019 Tommy John surgery. They gave him first-round money to eschew his commitment to Vanderbilt. He's quite a few years away, but his talent is promising.

Braxton Garrett LHP
Born: 08/05/97   Age: 23   Bats: L   Throws: L
Height: 6'2"   Weight: 202   Origin: Round 1, 2016 Draft (#7 overall)

YEAR	TEAM	LVL	AGE	W	L	SV	G	GS	IP	H	HR	BB/9	K/9	K	GB%	BABIP
2019	JUP	HI-A	21	6	6	0	20	20	105	92	13	3.2	10.1	118	53.9%	.294
2019	JAX	AA	21	0	1	0	1	1	1^2	4	0	16.2	5.4	1	55.6%	.444
2020	MIA	MLB	22	1	1	0	2	2	7^2	8	3	5.9	9.4	8	61.9%	.278
2021 FS	MIA	MLB	23	2	2	0	57	0	50	47	6	4.6	8.3	46	47.5%	.290
2021 DC	MIA	MLB	23	1	1	0	4	4	19.3	18	2	4.6	8.3	17	47.5%	.290

Comparables: Pedro Avila, Trevor Rogers, Jonathan Hernández

Garrett tore his UCL only four games into his pro career back in 2017, which cost him nearly all of his first two full seasons. He took the ball on his regular turn in 2019, reestablishing his health and a solid level of performance. What he didn't quite have was his best fastball velocity, but that sometimes lags a year behind the return to the field. He didn't get the expected chance to establish his best fastball in the minors in 2020, and when called upon for a pair of spot starts in the majors it was still hovering right around 90. While Garrett still has a plus curveball and a strong command profile, he's going to have a hard time missing many bats without a little more oomph on the fastball and better velocity separation between his heater and change. We remain hopeful that will all come around with a better foundation; he's still only 129 2/3 innings into his pro career, after all.

YEAR	TEAM	LVL	AGE	WHIP	ERA	DRA-	WARP	MPH	FB%	WHF	CSP
2019	JUP	HI-A	21	1.23	3.34	99	0.2				
2019	JAX	AA	21	4.20	16.20	209	-0.1				
2020	MIA	MLB	22	1.70	5.87	103	0.1	90.9	48.9%	23.1%	
2021 FS	MIA	MLB	23	1.46	4.49	103	0.2	90.9	48.9%	23.1%	37.0%
2021 DC	MIA	MLB	23	1.46	4.49	103	0.2	90.9	48.9%	23.1%	37.0%

Miami Marlins 2021

Jorge Guzman RHP
Born: 01/28/96   Age: 25   Bats: R   Throws: R
Height: 6'1"   Weight: 246   Origin: International Free Agent, 2014

YEAR	TEAM	LVL	AGE	W	L	SV	G	GS	IP	H	HR	BB/9	K/9	K	GB%	BABIP
2018	JUP	HI-A	22	0	9	0	21	21	96	84	7	6.0	9.5	101	37.9%	.308
2019	JAX	AA	23	7	11	0	25	24	138²	96	13	4.6	8.2	127	31.7%	.244
2020	MIA	MLB	24	0	0	0	1	0	1	2	2	9.0	0.0	0	20.0%	.000
2021 FS	MIA	MLB	25	2	3	0	57	0	50	48	9	5.9	8.4	46	33.1%	.285
2021 DC	MIA	MLB	25	3	3	0	33	3	38.3	37	6	5.9	8.4	36	33.1%	.285

Comparables: Matt Hall, Mauricio Llovera, Keury Mella

Guzman popped up for an emergency August cameo by virtue of already being on the 40-man roster, where he showed off the good (upper-90s heater and two viable secondary offerings) and bad (poor command) in his lone relief appearance. He appears headed down the bullpen path long-term.

YEAR	TEAM	LVL	AGE	WHIP	ERA	DRA-	WARP	MPH	FB%	WHF	CSP
2018	JUP	HI-A	22	1.54	4.03	101	0.5				
2019	JAX	AA	23	1.20	3.50	85	1.3				
2020	MIA	MLB	24	3.00	18.00	131	0.0	98.8	63.2%	0.0%	
2021 FS	MIA	MLB	25	1.63	5.67	122	-0.4	98.8	63.2%	0.0%	47.0%
2021 DC	MIA	MLB	25	1.63	5.67	122	-0.3	98.8	63.2%	0.0%	47.0%

Brandon Leibrandt LHP
Born: 12/13/92   Age: 28   Bats: L   Throws: L
Height: 6'4"   Weight: 190   Origin: Round 6, 2014 Draft (#172 overall)

YEAR	TEAM	LVL	AGE	W	L	SV	G	GS	IP	H	HR	BB/9	K/9	K	GB%	BABIP
2018	LHV	AAA	25	4	1	0	20	6	50²	34	1	1.8	5.7	32	46.6%	.229
2020	MIA	MLB	27	0	0	0	5	0	9	3	0	7.0	3.0	3	38.5%	.115
2021 FS	MIA	MLB	28	2	3	0	57	0	50	50	8	3.4	6.8	37	40.6%	.285

Comparables: Andrew Suárez, William Cuevas, Tyler Wilson

The Marlins looked absolutely everywhere for major-league ready players after they lost most of their roster to COVID. They found Leibrandt pitching for the New Jersey Blasters, a Washington Generals-style house opponent the Somerset Patriots formed to have a team to play against in the absence of an Atlantic League season. After years of struggling with injuries, the former Phillies prospect made the majors just a few short weeks later, although the story has an unhappy ending—he went down for the season with another elbow injury after just five appearances.

YEAR	TEAM	LVL	AGE	WHIP	ERA	DRA-	WARP	MPH	FB%	WHF	CSP
2018	LHV	AAA	25	0.87	1.42	83	0.7				
2020	MIA	MLB	27	1.11	2.00	127	-0.1	90.6	47.3%	14.7%	
2021 FS	MIA	MLB	28	1.40	4.66	107	0.1	90.6	47.3%	14.7%	50.5%

Max Meyer   RHP
Born: 03/12/99   Age: 22   Bats: L   Throws: R
Height: 6'0"   Weight: 196   Origin: Round 1, 2020 Draft (#3 overall)

With great rotation upside comes great bullpen risk. The Marlins bypassed safer options like Texas A&M lefty Asa Lacy and Vanderbilt slugger Austin Martin with the third pick last summer in favor of Meyer's venomous two-pitch combo. The converted closer was hitting triple digits as a starter with his lively fastball during the abbreviated 2020 college season, and his hard slider has as much bite as any in the game. The changeup needs work—he didn't need it a whole lot as a Minnesota Golden Gopher—and if it doesn't get there he's going back into the bullpen-verse sooner or later. Frankly, we half-expected to see him slinging webs out of the 'pen in the playoffs a la Garrett Crochet. He's a kingpin-in-waiting if he can stick as a starter, and you know, one grade of changeup really can make a difference.

Drew Rucinski   RHP
Born: 12/30/88   Age: 32   Bats: R   Throws: R
Height: 6'2"   Weight: 190   Origin:

YEAR	TEAM	LVL	AGE	W	L	SV	G	GS	IP	H	HR	BB/9	K/9	K	GB%	BABIP
2018	NO	AAA	29	0	0	0	14	0	25	27	0	2.2	7.6	21	57.3%	.365
2018	MIA	MLB	29	4	2	0	32	0	35^1	34	2	3.3	6.9	27	47.3%	.299
2019	NC	KBO	30	9	9	0	30	30	177^1	164	13	2.0	6.0	119		
2020	NC	KBO	31	19	5	0	30	30	183	173	14	2.0	8.2	167		
2021									No projection							

Comparables: César Ramos, Justin Grimm, Joe Biagini

Most of the international pitchers in the KBO are spot starters, or at the very least Triple-A workhorses. Rucinski was thus an odd choice for the Dinos to pursue, as the right-hander had barely started at all in his past five seasons. The gamble proved a masterstroke, as Rucinski quickly became one of the league's top arms and the driving force behind the club's Korean Series victory. The right-hander started twice, winning both games, and also pitched three innings of dominant relief in Game 4 to even the series at two apiece. He may not have planned to become Korea's Madison Bumgarner, but it's certainly not a bad life to stumble into.

Miami Marlins 2021

YEAR	TEAM	LVL	AGE	WHIP	ERA	DRA-	WARP	MPH	FB%	WHF	CSP
2018	NO	AAA	29	1.32	2.52	56	0.7				
2018	MIA	MLB	29	1.33	4.33	92	0.3	95.2	48.1%	23.9%	
2019	NC	KBO	30	1.18	3.05						
2020	NC	KBO	31	1.26	3.05						
2021						No projection					

Josh D. Smith   LHP

Born: 10/11/89   Age: 31   Bats: L   Throws: L
Height: 6'3"   Weight: 200   Origin: Round 25, 2012 Draft (#766 overall)

YEAR	TEAM	LVL	AGE	W	L	SV	G	GS	IP	H	HR	BB/9	K/9	K	GB%	BABIP
2018	WOR	AAA	28	9	5	0	28	14	98^2	85	4	3.9	8.8	97	43.2%	.301
2019	COL	AAA	29	8	1	6	41	0	52^2	32	7	4.1	12.6	74	38.5%	.229
2019	MIA	MLB	29	0	0	0	6	0	4^1	3	0	6.2	4.2	2	26.7%	.200
2019	CLE	MLB	29	0	0	0	8	0	8^1	8	0	8.6	13.0	12	38.1%	.381
2020	MIA	MLB	30	0	0	0	2	0	1^2	2	1	5.4	21.6	4	33.3%	.500
2021 FS	MIA	MLB	31	2	3	0	57	0	50	46	7	5.1	10.2	56	40.0%	.305

Comparables: Adam Kolarek, Cole Sulser, Gregory Infante

On August 19th, 2020, lefty Josh A. Smith relieved righty Josh D. Smith for Miami, repeating a trick the early-2000s Mets used to pull off where you pull one bad pitcher for another who has the same name but throws with the opposite arm. Unlike the Bobbies Jones, it doesn't seem like these two are going to stay in the majors long enough to pull it off again.

YEAR	TEAM	LVL	AGE	WHIP	ERA	DRA-	WARP	MPH	FB%	WHF	CSP
2018	WOR	AAA	28	1.30	3.01	88	1.2				
2019	COL	AAA	29	1.06	2.73	49	1.9				
2019	MIA	MLB	29	1.38	8.31	161	-0.1	91.4	61.8%	21.6%	
2019	CLE	MLB	29	1.92	5.40	103	0.0	92.4	62.8%	21.3%	
2020	MIA	MLB	30	1.80	10.80	70	0.0	90.5	67.4%	30.8%	
2021 FS	MIA	MLB	31	1.49	5.13	112	-0.1	92.0	63.4%	23.2%	49.1%

Marlins Prospects

The State of the System:
The Marlins might not be able to repeat their surprise playoff run in 2021, but they are well-positioned for next year and beyond with a deep pipeline of talent.

The Top Ten:

1 ★ ★ ★ *2021 Top 101 Prospect* **#4** ★ ★ ★

Sixto Sánchez **RHP** OFP: 70 ETA: Debuted in 2020
Born: 07/29/98 Age: 22 Bats: R Throws: R Height: 6'0" Weight: 234
Origin: International Free Agent, 2015

The Report: Sánchez has long been one of the hardest throwing prospects in baseball, and has long had a wide variety of other stuff with plus-or-better potential. He consistently sits in the upper-90s and touches higher with both his four-seam and two-seam fastballs, generating different looks and manipulating the pitches well, but with relatively below-average spin and more horizontal funk than vertical. For some years, we've been waiting for one or more of Sánchez's offspeed pitches to break out of a kitchen sink of above-average offerings that flashed plus. Frankly, he'd pitched to contact a lot in the minors, breezing through easily in terms of results by generating weak swings but never really burying hitters to the level you'd think given the fastball and multiple plus-flashing offspeeds.

Development Track: Well, the changeup got there. What was as recently as 2019 one of three "potential plus, flash plus-plus" offerings looked more like a steady plus-plus offering in the majors. The slider didn't look far off, either. Sánchez was one of the better pitchers in the majors after being called up in late-August—though once again without posting whiff rates commensurate with his stuff and overall performance—and he's pretty close to his OFP already. He's one of the best prospects in baseball.

Variance: Medium. As early as spring 2017 and as recently as yesterday, I have made arguments that Sánchez could be an 80 OFP because his 75th-percentile outcome is awful close to a true ace given the breadth and quality of stuff. There's enough against that to hold the line at a role 7 for now—health and durability concerns, occasionally wavering command, lack of elite swing-and-miss generation—but there's certainly more positive variance here than for your typical 70 OFP pitching prospect.

J.P. Breen's Fantasy Take: Sánchez has taken gargantuan steps forward. Folks had questioned whether his fastball could miss enough bats, and it had a 12.7 percent whiff rate in 2020. The fastball-changeup combination is good enough for a top-of-the-rotation profile, as noted above. However, without an improved slider, Sánchez has an eerily similar profile to Chris Paddack, who had a disappointing 2020 campaign, or even Kevin Gausman. The health concerns should also keep dynasty owners from pushing in all their chips. Make no mistake, though, Sánchez is one of the most exciting young pitchers in Major League Baseball, and few minor leaguers have his upside.

───── ★ ★ ★ *2021 Top 101 Prospect* **#33** ★ ★ ★ ─────

2

JJ Bleday   RF   OFP: 60   ETA: 2021
Born: 11/10/97   Age: 23   Bats: L   Throws: L   Height: 6'3"   Weight: 205
Origin: Round 1, 2019 Draft (#4 overall)

The Report: Bleday features one of the most well-rounded offensive profiles of any prospect, and could make contributions to the big league club very early in the 2021 season. He will offer the Marlins' lineup a combination of advanced bat-to-ball abilities for a slugger of his ilk, as he is able to get the barrel to the ball quickly with a quick left-handed stroke. The hands can get a bit bouncy with a whippy bat pre-release, still at a great firing position with a high elbow that creates plenty of loft in the swing, too, leading to plus power. As for another plus tool, he's a good fit for right field thanks to a plus arm that has both carry and accuracy to his throws. The hulking outfielder isn't exactly the speediest, which is perhaps the only knock against his game.

Development Track: Bleday was believed to have been penciled-in for a 2020 campaign in Double-A, and as such, hasn't played above A-ball. He got plenty of time this year at the Marlins' complex; still, he'll likely get some extra seasoning in the minors before leveling-up to the majors.

Variance: Low. He's done it at every level so far, showing a good eye at the plate and minimal swing-and-miss, all which add to the confidence with the outcome.

J.P. Breen's Fantasy Take: Bleday doesn't generate as much dynasty excitement as he should. He won't run much, and he hit just .257/.311/.379 in his professional debut. It's important to remember, though, that Bleday plied his trade in Jupiter, which is one of the least power-friendly ballparks in one of the least hitter-friendly leagues. Trust the scouting reports. Bleday still boasts one of the best power-average combinations in the minors. He's a top-200 dynasty player and a top-40 dynasty prospect.

★ ★ ★ *2021 Top 101 Prospect* **#45** ★ ★ ★

3
Edward Cabrera   RHP   OFP: 60   ETA: 2021
Born: 04/13/98   Age: 23   Bats: R   Throws: R   Height: 6'5"   Weight: 217
Origin: International Free Agent, 2015

The Report: Despite an early season outbreak of COVID-19 that decimated the Marlins' pitching staff, Cabrera was not among those called to fill the void. Not because of talent or readiness, but due to a bad case of timing with a minor injury. Those minor injuries—also experienced in 2019—have prevented him from skyrocketing up prospect lists, as evaluators resoundingly agree on the legit stuff exploding out of his right arm. When healthy, it's a lively fastball that cruises 95-97 and can even sit in the 97-99 range for extended periods. Both the breaking ball and changeup feature above average qualities; depending on the day one can seem superior over the other. The ease of the delivery and the finish on his pitches point toward an impact starter needing to shed pesky ailments to realize top-of-the-rotation potential.

Development Track: The Marlins have been consistent with their top-end pitching prospects, handling them with kid gloves to try and avoid any major complications as they matriculate out of the system. Cabrera has been on a familiar parallel path to Sánchez, only once eclipsing the 100-inning mark in a season. He could have easily been called up in 2020, and barring any further annoyances will get the call in 2021.

Variance: Medium. Everything is there to be a complete pitcher. What is missing is a track record over the course of a full season of major league sized workload.

J.P. Breen's Fantasy Take: Explosive fastball. Secondary pitches that can all flash plus, depending on the day. Some durability/health concerns. You'd be forgiven for thinking that this sounds a lot like Sixto Sánchez's write-up from 12 months ago. The right-hander is perhaps the best pitching prospect about whom no one is talking. He's an easy top-100 dynasty prospect for me, and I like the combination of scouting profile and organization enough to put him ahead of more heralded pitching prospects.

★ ★ ★ *2021 Top 101 Prospect* **#51** ★ ★ ★

4
Max Meyer   RHP   OFP: 60   ETA: 2022 as a reliever, 2023 as a starter
Born: 03/12/99   Age: 22   Bats: L   Throws: R   Height: 6'0"   Weight: 196
Origin: Round 1, 2020 Draft (#3 overall)

The Report: A strong showing for the Collegiate National Team put Meyer into first-round consideration for the 2020 draft. He had previously been the closer at the University of Minnesota before shifting to the weekend rotation his sophomore year, showing he could handle a starter's workload and then outright dominating his abbreviated draft year. Many of the questions regarding whether he's a future starter or reliever stem from his 6-foot stature. The Marlins took this into account, but inevitably sided with the pure arm talent over any height concerns. Using a fastball that rides comfortably in the mid-to-upper 90s and an upper 80s slider that one scout called, "the best I've seen in 20 years," it looks like a typical late-inning reliever profile. However, between his athletic, repeatable delivery, and two present plus pitches, Meyer has a good shot to break the obvious reliever mold and become a dynamic starter.

Development Track: Two questions will determine whether or not Meyer sticks in the rotation. Can his build hold up over the course of a season, and can the changeup develop into a usable third pitch? If both are answered in the affirmative, there is a little doubt he will end up as a starter. Failing those, he could be an elite closer with velocity readings reaching 100 and a slider that could be near-unhittable. Prior to the draft, the industry considered him a high variance player for valid reasons—some teams had him towards the back-half of the first round, and at least one had him at the top of their board. The Marlins believed his make-up, combined with the fastball/slider pairing, made him the easy choice at third overall.

Variance: High. It's not the ideal frame for a 30-start pitcher. There are plenty of examples of guys with similar builds who overcome the maxim that you need to be a certain height and weight to survive the rigors of a season. It's not uncommon, but Meyer will need to prove he's capable.

J.P. Breen's Fantasy Take: Meyer is a top-100 dynasty prospect, thanks to a dynamic slider that should lead to gaudy strikeout totals. If he can stick in the rotation, he's a 200-plus strikeout starter. If he transitions to the bullpen, the above scouting report suggests that he could be a top-10 fantasy closer with enough strikeouts to remain fantasy relevant as a non-closer. The latter currently seems more likely, and that's still a good enough fantasy arm that the SP3 upside makes him worth a first-round pick in offseason supplemental drafts.

─────── ★ ★ ★ *2021 Top 101 Prospect* **#58** ★ ★ ★ ───────

5 **Jazz Chisholm SS** OFP: 60 ETA: Debuted in 2020
Born: 02/01/98 Age: 23 Bats: L Throws: R Height: 5'11" Weight: 184
Origin: International Free Agent, 2015

The Report: The Marlins seemed to target loud tools and extreme variance profiles in trade as the Jeter-era began. Chisholm certainly fits the bill, although like the rest of this group, it hasn't all quite clicked at the plate for him yet. He has plus raw and plus bat speed that unfurls itself from a violent uppercut out of a noisy setup. There's better bat control than you'd think, but Chisholm can really sell out for pullside power, which exacerbates what will be at best above-average swing-and-miss. He may hit the ball hard enough, and grab enough infield hits, to make the hit tool play to average, but there's not much of a floor to his contact rate at present. In the field, he's a sure-handed, rangy shortstop with enough arm for the left side. Ultimately, how much Chisholm reins in his aggressive, free-swinging tendencies will determine the outcome, but plus regular remains a distinct possibility.

Development Track: Chisholm didn't exactly dominate Double-A in 2019, so it's not a surprise he struggled at times after he was promoted to the Fish from the alternate site. His playing time was also erratic, as he didn't really unseat Miguel Rojas or Jon Berti from the middle infield spots despite the pair's defensive flexibility. Chisholm never really got into a rhythm against major league arms, although the upside certainly. He could use some consolidation time in Triple-A in 2021, but he's not that far off a more permanent role with the Marlins, although the range of outcomes remains broad.

Variance: High. I wouldn't call his debut a disaster, but a 30 percent K-rate and 74 DRC+ doesn't exactly assuage concerns about how the bat will play against top-level pitching. Given the present speed, pop, and glove though, Chisholm should be able to carve out a decently long career even if it's only as a bench infielder.

J.P. Breen's Fantasy Take: Given the long-term questions regarding his hit tool, Chisholm appears poised to be a poor man's Javier Báez—exciting power, speed, and defense without the .280 batting average. Dynasty owners will need Chisholm to be a 20-20 guy to justify the poor average. Even then, he's not far from a Rougned Odor-type fantasy profile. Chisholm, for me, is a better real-life prospect than a dynasty one. His high strikeout rate and low batting average put too much pressure on his power and speed.

─────── ★ ★ ★ *2021 Top 101 Prospect* **#94** ★ ★ ★ ───────

6 **Trevor Rogers** **LHP** OFP: 60 ETA: Debuted in 2020
Born: 11/13/97 Age: 23 Bats: L Throws: L Height: 6'5" Weight: 217
Origin: Round 1, 2017 Draft (#13 overall)

The Report: I must admit that when we started our offseason list project, I was surprised to see Rogers pop up in strong 101 consideration. He's been a pretty high profile prospect for awhile, and what I saw as the season went along in the majors seemed pretty true to form to his pre-2020 profile, which was a level below that—a nice three-pitch starting prospect. Then I dug deeper.

Development Track: It turns out Rogers was a hell of a lot more impressive than I thought in the majors, making a bunch of incremental improvements off his previous profile that added up to significant development. His fastball averaged 94 mph, continuing a fairly consistent upward trend since his 2018 pro debut, and with quite a lot of spin attached too. His changeup looked plus and the slider wasn't far behind, both progressing along ahead of schedule. Rogers had an ugly ERA owing to a nightmare outing in Philadelphia, but overall he pitched well, with a shiny DRA and decent peripherals. He could use another half-grade of command and slider development, but given that he barely had 200 minor-league innings, this has already come together really fast. He's a 101 guy now.

Variance: Medium. Rogers has already shown up in the majors, and things are pointing in the right direction.

J.P. Breen's Fantasy Take: For as much as we've lauded Sixto Sánchez's changeup, Rogers had a better whiff rate than Sánchez on his changeup in 2020 (23.77 percent to 17.7 percent, respectively). He'll need to throw strikes more consistently to avoid an unattractive WHIP, but the lefty is one of the higher-upside arms among those who currently sit outside our Top-500 Dynasty Rankings.

7 Jesús Sánchez RF OFP: 55 ETA: Debuted in 2020
Born: 10/07/97 Age: 23 Bats: L Throws: R Height: 6'3" Weight: 222
Origin: International Free Agent, 2014

The Report: The overriding theme of our reports and list blurbs on Sánchez over the last few seasons has been: "Well he will have to hit, but we think he will hit." Carrying a corner outfield profile even as a teenager, Sánchez tore up the low minors while being young for his assignments. His combination of compact stroke, plus bat speed, and projectable strength made us confident he would hit—and hit the ball hard enough—to carry a corner outfield profile. The approach has always been on the aggressive side, but Sánchez generally had the bat control to make it work and do damage. He's fast enough to be fine in either corner, but not a major defensive asset.

Development Track: In August, Sánchez joined the litany of Marlins prospects pressed into MLB service in 2020. His 10 days in the majors did not go well, as he looked overmatched, his swing out of sorts and out of sync. Unlike several of his still prospect-eligible teammates, Sánchez has a fair amount of upper minors experience, including six weeks at Triple-A in 2019. And zooming out further, he hasn't really hit in the upper minors at all. There's still a chance Sánchez puts it all together, and the underlying ability is still there for a plus hit/power right fielder, but at a certain point the projection has to make its way into the real world. You don't want to ding him too much for 10 bad games in a weird season, but we often talk on the prospect team about whether it "looked right" in the majors. Sánchez didn't in 2020.

Variance: High. The question with Sánchez has always been when it would click at the plate and how loud it would be when it did. The longer it doesn't happen, the more you wonder if it ever will, and the swing-and-miss issues in the majors were stark enough to make you worry about the realistic floor.

J.P. Breen's Fantasy Take: The physical tools are loud, but the statistics are ugly. He has power projection but has not posted an ISO over .200 since 2016. And the ground-ball rate has been 50-plus percent. He has the tools to hit for average, if it all comes together, but he has only hit .275 at one stop since reaching Double-A in 2018. And now the strikeout rate has spiked. If Sánchez weren't a top-100 dynasty prospect, he might be worth a low-stakes gamble. As it stands, though, he looks to be Lewis Brinson with prospect eligibility. And that's not a compliment.

8 **Nasim Nunez** SS   OFP: 55   ETA: 2023
Born: 08/18/00   Age: 20   Bats: S   Throws: R   Height: 5'9"   Weight: 160
Origin: Round 2, 2019 Draft (#46 overall)

The Report: For a light-hitting shortstop to claw his way into the top 10 of a very deep and talented system, there must be some special talents to justify the ranking. In the case of Nunez, there's a series of skills that grade out towards the top of the scale. To start, he has elite plate discipline that allows him to get on base with an uncanny ability for his age. So even though his switch-hitting stroke lacks any sort of thump—and may never even get to below-average power—he should make enough contact and draw plenty of walks to buoy his on-base percentage. Which is where his second near-elite skill comes into play: his plus-plus speed and baserunning instincts makes him a terror on the base-paths for pitchers and catchers alike. And finally, and perhaps the most important of his positive traits, is a glove and arm that could contend for hardware in the future.

Development Track: The challenge for Nunez will be to add strength without putting too much of a damper on his straight-line speed. He has remained lean since his drafting, but has added some good weight to help with his durability and add some oomph at the plate. As he continues to advance and face better pitching, the foundation of hitting is there to improve the hit tool to a potentially average grade, which would lock him in as an everyday player.

Variance: High. It's all contingent on the bat and whether it's a liability, good enough, or better than hoped. If it's either of the last two options, he could be a special player.

J.P. Breen's Fantasy Take: Nunez is a great late-round target for supplemental drafts. He has a legitimate pathway to the big leagues and has category-carrying speed potential. If the batting average takes a positive step in 2021, we might be looking at the infield version of Cristian Pache. Oh, and after reading the above scouting report, I wanted to add this for my buddy Craig: Hardware.

9 **Dax Fulton** LHP   OFP: 55   ETA: 2024
Born: 10/16/01   Age: 19   Bats: L   Throws: L   Height: 6'6"   Weight: 230
Origin: Round 2, 2020 Draft (#40 overall)

The Report: Despite being injured during the tail-end of the summer showcase portion of his draft year, the book was already out on Fulton as one of the top lefty arms in the 2020 class. He's a monster for his age, standing 6-foot-6 with a solid build, a bit narrow-chested, but with overall a good frame. His height really allows for him to attack with his heater down in the zone, which he then follows up with a big breaking curveball that locks up hitters on their front foot. Like most high schoolers, he toyed around with a changeup which will eventually come into play. What's important is the projectable body and the potential for at least two plus pitches.

Development Track: It's never a good thing to have Tommy John surgery, especially during your draft year. The Marlins saw past Fulton's injury that occurred in late 2019, and in a way, couldn't have been hurt at a better time. Focusing on the rehab process during the pandemic will allow him to toe the rubber come 2021 without missing any games of consequence.

Variance: Extreme. Recently drafted 19-year-olds coming off TJ are about as far away from the majors as possible. Every pitcher recovers differently, and we need to see how things look in 2021 as he gets back into form. The eventual grade here could be off one or two standard deviations depending on the rehab and how he develops.

J.P. Breen's Fantasy Take: Prep arms are risky enough in dynasty. Add in the Tommy John surgery, and y'all don't need to bother until next winter. Even then, he's years away.

10 Peyton Burdick OF   OFP: 55   ETA: 2022
Born: 02/26/97   Age: 24   Bats: R   Throws: R   Height: 6'0"   Weight: 210
Origin: Round 3, 2019 Draft (#82 overall)

The Report: Some of the words that have been used to describe Burdick: "animal," "beast," "bulldog," among other monstrous varieties. The former third-round pick out of Wright State parlayed a productive summer at the Cape into an eye-popping stat line the following spring, walking nearly twice as much as he struck out, clobbering 15 homers, and stealing 24 bases. Seamlessly transitioning to pro ball, he continued his mashing ways as one of the most productive hitters in Low-A. At 6-foot, he's not the towering individual you'd expect to be launching majestic home runs, but he's good at using his stout lower half and jacked arms to generate power from a balanced swing.

Development Track: Continuing the nickname barrage, "gym rat" and "workout warrior" can also be added to the list. He's received high praise for his work ethic and makeup, forcing his way into the discussion to be part of a crowded future outfield. As long as he continues to adjust to each new level of pitching, there is little tangible development left to make beyond those adjustments.

Variance: Medium. As hot as Burdick was for all of 2019, you hate to have anything prevent you from continuing that streak. After the layoff, if he comes out on fire yet again, we'll know just how for real he is, with a 55 potentially being on the low end of outcomes.

J.P. Breen's Fantasy Take: Burdick has been a trendy name in the dynasty community for the past 12-14 months. He's a top-200 dynasty prospect and could skyrocket up lists with a strong 2021 campaign. Word to the wise: Pay attention to how successful he is stealing bases next season. He stole seven bags in 2019 but was caught seven times. If that ratio doesn't improve, he won't be a double-digit steal threat at the big-league level, as no manager will give him the green light enough to matter.

The Prospects You Meet Outside The Top Ten

Top Ten Prospects in a shallower system

Braxton Garrett   LHP   Born: 08/05/97   Age: 23   Bats: L   Throws: L   Height: 6'2"   Weight: 202   Origin: Round 1, 2016 Draft (#7 overall)

It's been a long year, but that's only part of the reason it feels like it's been ages since Garrett was the seventh overall draft pick. The elevator pitch for him as a top 10 talent was "second-best lefty curve in the draft." Which means plus-plus potential when you are only beat out by Jay Groome Garrett missed 2018 with Tommy John surgery, but the curve remains a pristine plus hook. The pitch got some foolish swings from major league hitters, but it's a below-average fastball in terms of both velocity and movement, so Garrett will have to walk a fine line as a starter. An improving change-up gives him a chance to be at least an average one though.

Kameron Misner   OF   Born: 01/08/98   Age: 23   Bats: L   Throws: L   Height: 6'4"   Weight: 218   Origin: Round 1, 2019 Draft (#35 overall)

A conundrum of a prospect before he was drafted, Misner has obvious physical tools but lacked the college production to back it up. With his size, speed, and lofty swing you'd expect him to put up big power and stolen base numbers, but they've been modest relative to what you see on video. Misner routinely puts together professional at-bats, but it's a borderline passive approach, attempting to get into counts where he can sit on a pitch and location to jump on. He maintained that strategy at instructs while playing all three outfield positions and is referred to often as a potentially dynamic player.

Major League-ready bats, but less upside than you'd like

Lewin Díaz   1B   Born: 11/19/96   Age: 24   Bats: L   Throws: L   Height: 6'4"   Weight: 217   Origin: International Free Agent, 2013

Díaz made the top 10 last year, and also was awfully close this year. The system improved around him, but he also badly flopped in a short major-league trial. He's a power-hitting first baseman who had a breakout 2019; he's hurt by not having the consolidation year in 2020. We expect him to get another shot at MLB

Miami Marlins 2021

time in 2021, but even though he adds some value as a good defender and has some hit tool potential, the margins to be an everyday first baseman remain tight.

Prospects to dream on a little

José Devers SS Born: 12/07/99 Age: 21 Bats: L Throws: R Height: 6'0" Weight: 174 Origin: International Free Agent, 2016
Devers was just 20 for the entire 2020 season. He didn't make his MLB debut, but he wasn't overmatched at all at the alternate site, enough that he was on the MLB taxi squad down the stretch. He's an above-average defender with promising bat-to-ball and pitch selection, and he runs well too. The profile is limited by a lack of power, but he'd have made most Top 10s, and he's deceptively close to the majors for a 21-year-old who has never played in the high-minors.

Osiris Johnson SS Born: 10/18/00 Age: 20 Bats: R Throws: R Height: 6'0" Weight: 181 Origin: Round 2, 2018 Draft (#53 overall)
As has been often referenced, those who missed a lot of time prior to 2020 really needed to take advantage of the opportunities afforded to them at either the alternate site or instructs. Having lost his 2019 season due to injury, Johnson turned heads this fall with a clean bill of health allowing his elite bat-speed to finally recover to pre-injury form. Still maturing into his 20-year-old body, Johnson is likely to be shifted over to third base next season where his offensive profile and arm strength should work just fine.

Connor Scott OF Born: 10/08/99 Age: 21 Bats: L Throws: L Height: 6'3" Weight: 187 Origin: Round 1, 2018 Draft (#13 overall)
The former first-round pick hasn't been mentioned in the same breath as the other members of his 2018 prep class (Jarred Kelenic, Nolan Gorman, Jordyn Adams, Triston Casas, etc.) yet Scott has been steadily improving outside of the spotlight. With average future hit and power tools—and more potentially more to come with minor swing tweaks—he also offers plus speed and a plus glove patrolling center field.

Top Talents 25 and Under (as of 4/1/2021):

1. Sixto Sánchez, RHP
2. Sandy Alcantara, RHP
3. Pablo Lopez, RHP
4. JJ Bleday, OF
5. Edward Cabrera, RHP
6. Max Meyer, RHP
7. Jazz Chisholm SS

8. Trevor Rogers, LHP
9. Isan Díaz, 2B
10. Elieser Hernandez, RHP

Folks, the Marlins might be good for awhile. Sandy Alcantara would be the most promising young pitcher for the majority of MLB organizations. He's a present mid-rotation innings eater with an All-Star nod under his belt already. The upper-90s heat and three average-or-better offspeeds hint at even more, if he can take the final steps.

Pablo López would be the most promising young pitcher in many organizations. He's always had plus command, but he's picked up velocity in the majors, and he's found a real out pitch in a changeup that he spammed almost 30 percent of the time. The entire 2020 MLB season was a short sample, granted, but López was seventh in pitching WARP, with most of the names in front of him being established aces.

Isan Díaz opted out of the season during the Marlins' COVID-19 outbreak. He opted back in right before the trade deadline, only to suffer a season-ending groin injury right after his return. Díaz still has big power potential, but he hasn't had much of a MLB opportunity yet and hasn't hit for average when he has. His stock will likely be way up or way down depending on how his 2021 goes.

Elieser Hernandez slides onto the back of this list in place of Jordan Yamamoto, whose 2020 never much got going at all. Hernandez, a former Rule 5 pick, is a homer-prone fastball/slider type who seems to be settling in well as a fourth or fifth starter.

Part 3: Featured Articles

Marlins All-Time Top 10 Players

by Matthew Trueblood

POSITION PLAYERS

J.T. REALMUTO, C (2014–2018)
Catchers are not supposed to be as athletic as Realmuto. In most cases, there's a strong case to be made that that athleticism is a bit wasted behind the plate. It's true that Realmuto's bat, despite flashes of brilliance, took longer to develop because of his position, and that his speed can't impact the game while he's in a squat. Still, he blossomed into the best catcher in the game, with an extremely quick release and top-shelf arm, a sufficiently balanced offensive skill set to post a 122 DRC+ in 2018, and leadership skills. In trade, he brought Sixto Sánchez, who the Marlins hope is their next ace.

JEFF CONINE, 1B/LF (1993–1997, 2003–2005)
Coming in as an expansion draftee, Conine played all 162 games in the Marlins' inaugural season. After that, the nickname "Mr. Marlin" was almost unavoidable. He was more solid than star-caliber and could be a bit inconsistent, but he spent almost a decade and a half finding ways to be an average player. He spent time at all four corner positions, earned a reputation as a leader, and was important to both Marlins championship teams.

LUIS CASTILLO, 2B (1996–2005)
Despite an almost incredible dearth of power Castillo was a valuable player. He matured into a Gold Glove-winning second baseman, learning to use his speed to cover ground better as he reached his mid-20s. His offensive game was all about speed on the surface, but was driven from beneath by great contact skills and good plate discipline. Despite posing little threat to drive the ball, he worked enough walks to run a .379 OBP from 1999 through 2005. There hasn't been a peskier hitter since his debut.

DAN UGGLA, 2B (2006–2010)

The last great Rule 5 draftee before eligibility for that draft was pushed back in 2006, Uggla was an instant success in Florida—as all Rule 5 draftees must be if they're to stick. Packing hilariously thick biceps and pectorals into normal-sized jerseys, Uggla looked like a first baseman or designated hitter and sometimes played the keystone like one. He averaged an extra-base hit every 10 plate appearances during his five seasons with the Marlins, though, and walked even more often, making him a deserving two-time All-Star.

MIKE LOWELL, 3B (1999–2005)

Five good seasons will get you into the Marlins Hall of Fame, and that's pretty much what Lowell, who came over from the Yankees in a steal of a trade, had to offer. He was a solid-average (but never dazzling) glove man at third base. From 2002 through 2004, he did mature into a borderline All-Star, as he started walking more and lifting the ball, but he largely made his bones with a quick bat, dead-pull approach, and the ability to work the count without striking out much. When he was the second- or third-best player in a lineup, it was usually a very good lineup.

MIGUEL CABRERA, 3B/1B/OF (2003–2007)

It's scary to reflect that Cabrera didn't peak until after the Marlins traded him—scary, because if he'd never gotten any better, the Tigers would still have been thrilled to get him. His power was incredible, right from the start, but the truly awe-inspiring thing about Cabrera has always been his ability to take good, perfectly-executed pitches, some of them even outside the strike zone, and absolutely annihilate them. In trade, he brought the team Andrew Miller and Cameron Maybin, but they couldn't begin to even up the loss. In the past it would have been scandalous for a team to trade a future triple crown winner, but not only was parting with Cabrera accepted as a rite of passage in Marlins existence, it's now more or less normal practice for all teams to deaccession stars they would previously have felt obligated to retain.

HANLEY RAMÍREZ, SS (2006–2012)

Packing value most players would be thrilled to compile over an entire career into his first five seasons, Ramírez never had another great, healthy season. He was 26 in 2010, and already an MVP-caliber shortstop with an elite power-speed blend. Then, in 2011, lower back trouble started. A shoulder injury on a diving play at shortstop required surgery. For 2012, the Marlins hired Ozzie Guillén, signed José Reyes, and moved Ramírez to third base. That sequence of choices led to a disgruntled, out-of-shape, disappointing Ramírez, and hastened his departure from town. He never stayed healthy enough to replicate his early brilliance, although there were glimpses of his old excellence right through to the end.

CLIFF FLOYD, OF (1997–2002)

When he was healthy Floyd could rake with a powerful swing and picturesque finish not unlike that of Ken Griffey, Jr. He slugged .523 during his Marlins tenure, his longest and best with any team, and had underrated speed on the bases. In right field, he might as well have spent his time practicing that stylish swing, but he still delivered plenty of value whenever he could stay on the field. Health is a skill and it's one of the few Floyd didn't have.

GIANCARLO STANTON, OF (2010–2017)

One of the great nicknames in recent memory never quite stuck. In six separate tweets between 2012 and 2015, David Price told the world that he calls Stanton "create-a-player," because Stanton looks and moves like something out of a Madden player's imagination. It's a pitch-perfect comparison. The mountainous right fielder only had three full, healthy seasons with the Fish, but hit 130 home runs during them, was worth 19.4 WARP, and had an aggregate DRC+ of 150. Alas, because of the team's mismanagement and miserliness, trading him away brought no impact talent in return.

CHRISTIAN YELICH, OF (2013–2018)

Whatever their faults, the Marlins have generally been great at amateur scouting. They found Yelich in the back half of 2010's first round despite choosing out one of the weakest draft classes of the last 30 years. They helped him smooth out an already-sweet swing and sowed the seeds from which he would eventually reap phenomenal power. His lankiness and consistency lulled them into missing the potential that he could turn the corner and become an MVP, though, which is an indictment of their coaching and development staff at the big-league level.

PITCHERS

KEVIN BROWN, RHP (1996–1997)

That Brown ranks high on this list despite pitching for Florida for just two seasons says volumes about the team and arguably even more about the man. Even so, that he's not in the Hall of Fame speaks almost solely to the foolishness of the voters. Brown was comfortable changing arm angles with almost all his pitches. He had a deceptive, hip-turning delivery, got remarkable extension, and was especially devastating with his S-suite: Sinker, splitter, and slider, all of which he could manipulate in various ways and none of which permitted hitters to lift the ball at all. He pitched 470 innings and was worth 15.6 WARP in those two years with the Fish.

ALEX FERNANDEZ, RHP (1997–2000)

Signing Fernandez in December 1996 was the Marlins' biggest single step from expansion team to legitimate contender even if they would turn back just a year later. He averaged over 5.0 WARP per season in the four preceding years, and he delivered another brilliant season in 1997. Then, right in the middle of Florida's championship run, he blew out his shoulder. Labrum surgery canceled his 1998 and ruined every subsequent season.

A.J. BURNETT, RHP (1999–2005)

For most of his Marlins career, Burnett was too wild to be truly dominant but on any given night he had the potential to perform at that level. He literally wore his influences and ambitions on his sleeve, wearing no. 34 and trying his damnedest to be Nolan Ryan. When he humped up, Burnett could scrape triple digits with his heat, and his curveball was a knee-buckler. He finally learned how to pitch, and had most of his best years, after leaving Florida.

BRAD PENNY, RHP (2000–2004)

Like Ricky Nolasco below, Penny looked like a guy who would throw much harder than he did. His control wandered and he would seem to pitch through nagging injuries for long periods, leading to inconsistency of every kind. Ultimately, though, he had a solid fastball-curveball combination. The Marlins traded him before he could develop his changeup and command enough to reach his full potential, but as it turned out, they only missed out on a mid-rotation starter, anyway.

JOSH BECKETT, RHP (2001–2005)

Not counting his star turn in the 2003 postseason, Beckett made only 103 starts and pitched 609 innings for the Marlins. When he came up, he sat in the upper 90s, and could either backspin his fastball at the top of the zone or sink it in on right-handed batters, with ridiculous movement. His fearlessness, so much on display during that 2003 run, allowed him to age gracefully, despite a litany of injuries that were nagging him even as he broke into the majors.

DONTRELLE WILLIS, LHP (2003–2007)

The physical charisma of a great, idiosyncratic pitcher is timeless. The world fell in love with Willis as eagerly as they had with Juan Marichal, Luis Tiant, and Fernando Valenzuela and with good reason. That Willis was also a great all-around athlete, capable of occasionally coming up with a big hit, and that his smile made him instantly marketable were delightful perks. His peak was incredibly short, but while it lasted, that high leg kick and his baffling spin kept everyone glued to their TVs.

JOSH JOHNSON, RHP (2005–2012)

Johnson became his generation's best example of the "healthy or hurt" pitching trope, but the latter won out too many times. Still, he won the ERA title in 2010, edging out Roy Halladay at a time when Halladay seemed unbeatable. Huge and strapping, Johnson had no frills. He threw a fastball that sat comfortably at 96 miles per hour, could sink it when he needed to, and owned perhaps the best slider in the National League. He just couldn't stay on the mound.

ANÍBAL SÁNCHEZ, RHP (2006–2012)

In the popular imagination, Sánchez only broke out as a co-ace after being traded to the Tigers in 2012. It's true that his first four seasons with Florida were marred by injuries and inconsistency. In 2010 and 2011, though, he turned a corner, with 195 innings one season, 196 the next, and earned a total of 8.1 WARP. He cleaned up his mechanics, firmed up his slider, and threw more strikes. As his strong start to 2012 proved, he was well on his way to stardom before being dealt to Detroit.

RICKY NOLASCO, RHP (2006–2013)

Nolasco came along at the end of a generation of big, hard-throwing young Marlins starters. He was equally big but never threw nearly as hard. Perhaps because of that, and even (perversely) because of his great control, he was always frustratingly unable to generate topline results in line with his excellent peripheral numbers. From 2008-11, he had a 75 DRA-, but a 4.41 ERA. Despite some good seasons and gaudy strikeout-to-walk ratios, he never really shook the problem.

JOSÉ FERNÁNDEZ, RHP (2013–2016)

We were given only a glimpse of a baseball world in which Fernández could be his best, brightest self, but it was a ray of sunshine that left warmth even in the darkness that followed. At the time, the team's decision not to manipulate Fernández's service time at the start of 2013 counted as unusual and was even derided. In hindsight, it gave us a few extra starts to witness his electric three-pitch mix and irrepressible, infectious, joyous enthusiasm. The game is better for that.

A Taxonomy of 2020 Abnormalities

by Rob Mains

I'm going to start this with a trivia question. Trust me, it's relevant. Don't bother skipping to the end of the article to find the answer, it's not there.

Only five players have appeared in 140 or more games for 16 straight seasons. Who are they?

It's a trivia question starting off an essay, so you know how this works: Whatever you guessed, you're wrong. It's okay. As someone who purchased this book, chances are good that you're an educated baseball fan. But the circumstances behind 2020 force us to abandon, or at least seriously question, some of our favorite patterns and crutches for evaluating the game we love.

We just completed what was undoubtedly the strangest season in MLB history. No fans, geographically limited schedule, universal DH, seven-inning twin bills, runners on second in extra innings, a 16-team postseason, a club playing at a Triple-A stadium. Some of these changes will likely persist (sorry), but we've never had so many tweaks dumped on us all at once, at least not since they figured out how many balls were in a walk.

And the biggest, of course, was the 60-game season. The 19th century was dotted with teams that went bankrupt before the season ended, but the lone season with only 60 scheduled games was 1877. That year there were only six teams, the league rostered a total of 77 players (just 16 more than the 2020 Marlins), and batters called for pitches to be thrown high or low by the pitcher, who was 50 feet away. We can say the 2020 season was easily the shortest ever for recognizable baseball.

As such, it'll stand out. Few abbreviated seasons do. Just about everybody reading this knows the 1994 season ended after Seattle's Randy Johnson struck out Oakland's Ernie Young for the last out of the Mariners-A's game on August 11. The ensuing player strike wiped out the rest of the season and the postseason. Teams played only 112-117 games that year.

And many of you know that a strike in the middle of the 1981 season split the season in two, resulting in the only Division Series until 1995. Teams played only 103-111 games that year, the shortest regular season since 1885.

Those two seasons are memorable. So when we see that nobody drove in 100 runs in 1981, or that Greg Maddux was the only pitcher with 180 or more innings pitched in 1994, we think, "Of course. Strike year."

But we don't remember other short years. You might not recall that the 1994 strike spilled into the next year, chopping 18 games off the 1995 schedule. You might've read that the 1918 season, played during the last pandemic, ended after Labor Day due to the government's World War I "work or fight" order. A strike erased the first week and a half of the 1972 season, but that year's best known as the last time pitchers batted in the American League.

The point is, while we don't remember small changes to the schedule, we remember the big ones. The 1981 mid-season strike. The 1994 season- and Series-ending strike. And, of course, the pandemic-shortened 2020 season. We won't need a reminder why Marcell Ozuna's 18 homers were the fewest to lead the National League in a century. (Literally; Cy Williams led with 15 in 1920.)

Now, about that trivia question. The five players are Hank Aaron, Brooks Robinson, Pete Rose, Ichiro Suzuki, and Johnny Damon. The one nobody gets, of course, is Damon, and a lot of people miss Ichiro, whose last season of 140-plus games came garbed in the red-orange and ocean blue of Miami when he was 42. That's half of what makes it a good question. The other half is the two guys whom many think made the list but didn't. Lou Gehrig? His streak started in the Yankees' 42nd game of the 1925 season and lasted only 13 seasons after that. And everybody assumes Cal Ripken Jr. did it, having played 2,632 straight games over 17 seasons. But one of those 17 seasons was 1994, when the Orioles played only 112 games.

My point? *I just told you* everybody remembers the 1994 strike year, but everybody forgets it fell in the middle of Ripken's streak, separating the first twelve years from the last four. Just because we recall something doesn't mean it's always at the front of our minds.

Nobody is going to forget 2020, and baseball is obviously not the main reason. But there will come a time in the future when you're looking at a player's or a team's record, and there will be baffling numbers there for 2020, and you'll think, "I wonder what happened." (Not to mention the missing line for minor league players.) Just like you forgot that the 1994 strike limited Ripken to 112 games.

Try not to forget it, though. The 2020 season resulted in weird statistical results for several reasons.

There were only 60 games.
I know, duh. But that had impacts beyond counting stats like Ozuna's home run total or Yu Darvish and Shane Bieber leading the majors with eight wins. (I know, pitcher wins, but still.)

The 162-game season is the longest among major North American sports, and that duration gives us a gift. Over the course of a long season, small variations tend to even out. A player who has a ten-game hot streak will probably have a ten-game cold streak. A team that starts the year losing a bunch of close games will probably win a bunch of them. We get regression to the mean. Statistics stabilize.

Consider flipping a coin. Over the long run, we expect it to come up heads about half the time. But the fewer flips, the more variation there'll be. If you flip a coin six times, probability theory tells us you'll get at least two-third heads about 34 percent of the time. Flip it 30 times, your chance of two-thirds heads drops to five percent.

Or, relevant to this case, if you flip a coin 60 times, your chance of getting at least 36 heads—that's 60 percent—is 7.75 percent. Expand the coin-flipping to 162 times, and the chance of getting 60 percent heads drops to 0.73 percent.

In other words, the odds of an outcome that's 20 percent better (or worse) than expected is *more than ten times higher* when you flip your coin 60 times than when you do it 162 times. Call it small sample size, call lack of mean reversion, or call it luck not evening out, 162 is a lot more predictive than 60. You get much more variation over 60 games than over 162. Bieber's 1.63 ERA and 0.87 FIP aren't something we'd see over a full season, and neither is Javier Baéz's .203/.238/.360.

Some players' lines in 2020 look normal. Brian Anderson had an .811 OPS in 2019 and an .810 OPS in 2020. (He probably would have gotten that last point if he'd been given enough time.) But there are many like Bieber and Baéz, some of them from young players still establishing their talent levels. The answer to the question, "What went right or wrong for that guy in 2020?" is most likely "Nothing, it was just a 2020 thing."

Preseason training was abbreviated for hitters.

Every year, spring training drags. Players get tired of it, fans get tired of it, and you sure can tell sportswriters get tired of it. Yes, something to get everyone into shape is necessary, but does it really have to drag on for over a month? Can't we shorten it?

The 2020 season answered in the negative, at least for hitters. Warren Spahn is credited with saying that hitting is timing and pitching is upsetting timing. It appears nobody had his timing down after the abbreviated July summer camp. Through August 9—18 games into the season—MLB batters were hitting .230/.311/.395 with a .275 BABIP. That BABIP, had it held, would have been the lowest since 1968, the Year of the Pitcher. In recent years it's hovered around .300.

It didn't hold. Play returned to more normal levels the rest of the year: .249/.325/.425 with a .297 BABIP starting August 10. But batters whose play concentrated in those first two weeks wound up with ugly lines. Andrew

Benintendi went on the injured list with a season-ending rib cage strain on August 11. His final line: .103/.314/.128 in 14 games. Franchy Cordero went on the IL with a hamate bone fracture on August 9 and a .154/.185/.231 line. Even though he came back strong in a late September return, it was too late to repair his full-season numbers.

Preseason training was abbreviated for pitchers.
Every year, spring training drags. Players get tired of it, fans get tired of it ... wait, I already said that. But the abbreviated preseason was tough on pitchers, too. As noted, they had the upper hand coming out of the gate. But then they lost that hand. And then their arms, too.

The 2020 season was spread over 67 days. During those 67 days, 237 pitchers hit the Injured List, compared to 135 in the first 67 days of 2019. A lot of those IL stints, though, were COVID-19-related. Still, over the first 67 days of the 2019 season, there were 72 pitchers on the IL with arm injuries. That figure jumped to 110 in 2020, a 53 percent increase.

There are a number of factors contributing to pitcher arm injuries, ranging from usage to velocity, but it appears that attenuated preseason training played a role. A lot of pitchers had super-short seasons due to arm woes. Corey Kluber, Roberto Osuna, and Shohei Ohtani combined for seven innings, none after August 8. All suffered arm injuries. We'll never know whether they'd have fared better with a longer preseason, but we can guess how they probably feel.

Everybody played.
Rosters were set to expand from 25 to 26 in 2020, so even if we'd had a normal season, we'd have likely seen 2019's record of 1,410 players on MLB rosters broken. But due to the pandemic, rosters started the year at 30 and were cut to only 28. Add multiple COVID-19 absences and the revolving door caused by poor starts by hitters and a rash of pitcher arm injuries, and 1,289 players appeared in MLB games in 2020. The comparable figure over the first 67 days of the 2019 season was 1,109. That 16 percent increase works out to an average of six more players per team in 2020 compared to a similar slice of 2019. A future look back at 2020 rosters will include a lot of unfamiliar names.

Plus became a minus.
In advanced metrics, we adjust batter and pitcher performance for park and league/era variations. A plus sign appended to the end of a measure means that it's adjusted for park and league. It's scaled to an average of 100, with higher figures above average and lower figures below average. (Similarly, a metric with a minus is also park- and league-adjusted and scaled to 100, with lower values better.) Here at BP, our advanced measure of offensive performance is DRC+. Baseball-Reference has OPS+ and FanGraphs has wRC+.

Using park and league adjustments, we can compare Dante Bichette's 1995 Steroid Era season at pre-humidor Coors Field (.340/.364/.620, 40 homers, 128 RBI, MVP runner-up) with Jim Wynn's 1968 Year of the Pitcher season at the cavernous Astrodome (.269/.376/.474, 26 homers, 67 RBI, no MVP votes). It's not close. DRC+, OPS+, and wRC+ all give the nod to Wynn, handily. This is a useful tool. As my Baseball Prospectus colleague Patrick Dubuque tweeted last fall, "Please note that when I ask how you are, I am already adjusting for era."

The 2020 season messes up plus (and minus) stats for two reasons. First, the park adjustment was based on only 30 home games instead of the usual 81. Everything noted above regarding the short season applies, literally doubly, to park effect calculations. DRC+ uses a single-season park factor. OPS+ uses a three-year average and wRC+ five years. The figure for 2020 is suspect.

Second, OPS+ and wRC+ adjust for league: American and National. (DRC+ adjusts for opponent, regardless of league.) While there were two leagues in 2020, they were an artificial construct. To reduce travel, teams played opponents geographically, not based on league. There weren't two leagues, American and National. There were three, Western, Central, and Eastern.

That makes a difference because teams in the same league played in different run-scoring environments. AL teams scored 4.58 runs per game, NL teams 4.71. That's a small difference. But teams in the East scored 0.21 more runs per game (4.95) than teams in the West (4.74), and they both scored a lot more than Central teams (4.25). Adjusting for league misses that difference, so this book will be safe in that regard, but other sources may be distorted somewhat.

Not every game was a "game."
In 2020, the rising tide of strikeouts was finally stemmed. Strikeouts per team per game fell from 8.8 in 2019 to 8.7 in 2020. That marked the first decline after 14 straight annual increases.

In 2020, the rising tide of strikeouts rose higher. Batters struck out in 23.4 percent of plate appearances compared to 23.0 percent in 2019. That marked the 15th straight annual increase.

Both are true statements.

Because of two rule changes—seven-inning doubleheaders and runners on second in extra innings—games in 2020 were unprecedented in their brevity. There were 37.0 plate appearances per game in 2020. The only years with fewer were 1904 and 1906-1909. The average game in 2020 entailed 8.61 innings pitched, the fewest since 1899.

So when you see any per-game stats for 2020, you need to increase them by 3 or 4 percent to get them on equal footing with recent years.

Or, better, just ignore them. Last year happened. There were major league games contested between major league teams. But when you're looking at those physical or electronic baseball cards, when you're weaving narratives over why this young player's inevitable rise to stardom fell apart or why that old veteran rekindled his magic, don't linger on the 2020 line. It was just too weird.

Thanks to Lucas Apostoleris for research assistance.

—Rob Mains is an author of Baseball Prospectus.

Tranches of WAR

by Russell A. Carleton

We ask "replacement level" to be a lot of things. Sometimes contradictory things. Sometimes I wonder if we know what it even means anymore. The original idea was that it represented the level of production that a team could expect to get from "freely available talent", including bench players, minor leaguers, and waiver wire pickups. It created a common benchmark to compare everyone to, and for that reason, it represented an advancement well beyond what was available at the time. In fact, it created a language and a framework for evaluating players that was not just better but *entirely* different than what came before it.

But then we started mumbling in that language. The idea behind "wins above replacement" was one part sci-fi episode and one part mathematical exercise. Imagine that a player had disappeared before the season and suddenly, in an alternate timeline, his team would have had to replace him. The distance between him and that replacement line was his value. We need to talk about that alternate timeline.

Without getting too into 2:00 am "deep conversations" with extensive navel-gazing, it's worth thinking about why one player might not be playing, while another might.

- A player might not be playing because he has a short-term injury or his manager believes that he needs a day off.
- A player might not be playing because he has a longer-term injury that requires him to be on the injured list.

There's a difference here between these two situations. In particular, the first one generally *doesn't* involve a compensatory roster move, while the second one does. It's possible, though not guaranteed, that the person who will be replacing the injured/resting player would be the same in either case. That matters. Teams generally carry a spare part for all eight position players on the diamond, although in the era of a four-player bench, those spare parts usually are the backup plan for more than one spot.

Miami Marlins 2021

A couple of years ago, I posed a hypothetical question. Suppose that a team had two players in its system fighting for a fourth outfielder spot. One of them was a league average hitter, but would be worth 20 runs below average if allowed to play center field for a full season. One of them was a perfectly average fielder, but would be 15 runs below average as a hitter, if allowed to play an entire season. Which of the two should the team roster? It's tempting to say the second one, as overall, he is the better player. That misses the point. A league average hitter on the bench isn't just a potential replacement for an injured outfielder. He might also pinch hit for the light-hitting shortstop in a key spot. You keep the average hitter on the roster, even though he isn't a hand-in-glove fit for one specific place on the field, because being a bench player is a different job description than being a long-term fill-in for someone. If you find yourself in need of a longer-term fill-in, you can bring the other guy up from AAA.

When we're determining the value of an everyday player though, if he had disappeared before the season and a team would have had to replace his production, they likely would have done it with a player who was a long-term fill-in type because they would have had to replace a guy who played everyday. Maybe that's the same guy that they would have rostered on their bench anyway, but we don't know. It gets to the query of what we hope to accomplish with WAR. Are we looking for an accurate modeling of reality or are we looking for a common baseline to compare everyone to? Both have their uses, but they are somewhat different questions.

Let's talk about another dichotomy.

- A player might not be playing because he isn't very good and is a bench-level player.
- A player might not be playing because there is another player on the team who has a situational advantage that makes him the better choice today. The classic case of this is a handedness platoon. On another day, he might be a better choice.

When we think about player usage, I think we're still stuck in the model that there are starters and there are scrubs. We have plenty of words for bench players or reserves or backups or utility guys. We do still have the word "platoon" in our collective vocabulary, but in the age of short benches, it's hard to construct one. It's always been hard to construct them. You have to find two players who hit with different hands, have skill sets that complement each other, and probably play the same position. In the era of the short bench, one of them had probably better double as a utility player in some way. Baseball has a two-tiered language geared toward the idea of regulars and reserves. The fact that it was so easy for me to find plenty of synonyms for "a player whose primary function is to come into a game to replace a regular player if he is injured or resting" should tell you something.

I'm always one to look for "unspoken words" in baseball. What is it called when someone is both half of a platoon and the utility infielder? That guy exists sometimes, but he reveals himself in that role—usually by accident. We don't have a word for that, and whenever I find myself saying "we don't have a word for that", I look for new opportunities. What do you call it, further, when the job of being the utility infielder is decentralized across the whole infield with occasional contributions from the left fielder? It's not even a "super-utility" player. What happens when you build your entire roster around the idea that everyone will be expected to be a triple major?

⚾ ⚾ ⚾

I think someone else beat me to this one, and on a grand scale. Platoons work because we know that hitters of the opposite hand to the pitcher get better results than hitters of the same hand, usually to the tune of about 20 points of OBP. If you want to express that in runs, it usually comes out to somewhere around 10 to 12 runs of linear weights value prorated across 650 PA. But hang on a second, now let's say that we have two players who might start today, both of roughly equal merit with the bat. One has a handedness advantage, but is the worse fielder of the two. In that case, as long as his "over the course of a season" projection as a fielder at whatever position you want to slot him into is less than a 10-run drop from the guy he might replace, then he's a better option today.

We're not used to thinking of utility players as bat-first options, who would play below-average defense at three different infield positions. That guy might hook on as a 2B/3B/LF type (Howie Kendrick, come on down!) but teams usually think to themselves that they need as their utility infielder someone who "can handle" shortstop, the toughest of the infield spots to play. If someone can do that *and* hit well, he's probably already starting somewhere, so he's not available as a utility infielder. It's easier for those glove guys to find a job. In a world where the replacement for a shortstop *has to be* the designated utility infielder, that makes sense.

But as we talked about last week, we're living in a different world. The rate at which a replacement for a regular starter turns out to be *another starter* shifting over to cover has gone way up over the last five years. There was always some of it in the game, but this has been a supernova of switcheroos. Now if your second baseman is capable of playing a decent shortstop, that 2B/3B/LF guy can swap in. He's not actually playing shortstop, and maybe the defense suffers from the switch, but if he's got enough of a bat, he might outhit those extra fielding miscues. And in doing so, he is effectively your backup shortstop.

Somewhere along the lines, teams got hip to the idea of multi-positional play from their regulars. I've written before about how you can't just put a player, however athletic, into a new position and expect much at first. The data tell us that. Eventually, players can learn to be multi-positionalists, but it takes time, roughly on the order of two months, before they're OK. But there's a hidden message in there. If you give a player some reps at a new spot, he's a reasonably gifted athlete and somewhat smart and willing to learn, he could probably pick it up enough to get to "good enough," and it doesn't take forever. You just have to be purposeful about it. Maybe you get to the point where you can start to say "he's still below average but we could move him there and get another bat into the lineup, and it's a net win."

Teams have started to build those extra lessons into their player development program. It used to be seen as a mark of weakness to be relegated to "utility player" because that meant that you were a bench player (all those synonyms above come with a side of stigma). Now, it's a way of building a team. If you get a few reps in the minors (where it doesn't count) at a spot, you'll have at least played the spot at game speed before. There are limits to how far you can push that. A slow-footed "he's out in left field because we don't have the DH" guy is never going to play short, but maybe your third baseman can try second base and not look like a total moose out there.

⚾ ⚾ ⚾

Back to WAR. I'd argue that the world of starters and scrubs is slowly disintegrating, for good cause. In the event that a regular starter really does go down with an injury–ostensibly, the alternate universe scenario that WAR is attempting to model–it makes the team a little more resilient to replacing him. And the good news is that you're more likely to be able to replace him with the best of the bench bunch, rather than the third-best guy, because the best guy doesn't have to be an exact positional match for the guy who got hurt. And that's what the manager would want to do. He'd want to replace that long-term production, not with an amalgam of everyone else who played that position, but with the best guy available from his reserves.

Now this is still WAR. We still want to retain the principle that we should be measuring a player, and not his teammates. We need some sort of common baseline, and despite what I just said, we'll still need some sort of amalgam. To construct that, I give to you the idea of the tranche. The word, if you've not heard it before, refers to a piece of a whole that is somehow segmented off. It's often used in finance to talk about layers of a financial instrument.

Here, I want you to consider that there are 30 starters at each of the seven non-battery positions (catchers should have their own WAR, since only a catcher can replace a catcher). We can identify them by playing time, and we can futz around with the definition a little bit if we need to. Next, among those who aren't in that starting pool, we identify the top tranche of the 30 best bench players, which I would again identify by playing time, and then the second and third and fourth and so on. If a player were to disappear, his manager would probably want to take a guy from that top tranche of the bench to replace him. In a world where even the starters can slide around the field, that becomes more feasible.

We can take a look at that top tranche and say "How many of them showed that they are able to play (first, second, etc.)?" and therefore could have directly substituted for the starter? How many of them could have been a direct substitute for our injured player? We don't know whether one of them would be on *a specific* team, but we can say that 40 percent of the time, a manager would have been able to draw from tranche 1 in filling the role, and 35 percent from tranche 2. But on tranche 1, we can also look at how many of those players played a position that could have then shifted and covered for that spot. We'd need some eligibility criteria for all of this (probably a minimum number of games played) but it would just be a matter of multiplication. Shortstop would be harder to fill, and managers would probably be dipping a little further down in the talent pool, and so replacement level would be lower, as it is now.

Doing some quick analysis, I found that the difference in just batting linear weights (haven't even gotten into running or fielding) between tranche 1 and tranche 2 in 2019 was about 6.5 runs, prorated across 650 PA. Between tranche 1 and tranche 3, it's 10.8 runs. The ability to shift those plate appearances up the ladder has some real value.

This part is important. We can also give credit to starters for the positions that they showed an ability to play, even if they didn't play them (this is the guy fully capable of playing center, but who's in a corner because the team already has a good center fielder) because he allows a team to carry a player who hits like a left fielder to functionally be the team's backup center fielder. He facilitates that movement upward among the tranches. We can start to appreciate the difference between a left fielder who would never be able to hack it in center (and the compensatory move that his team would have to make) and the left fielder who could do it, but just didn't have to very often.

Past that, you can continue to use whatever hitting and fielding and running metrics you like to determine a player's value, but when we get down to constructing that baseline, I'd argue we need a better conceptual and mathematical framework. It's going to require some more #GoryMath than we're used to, but I'd argue it's a better conceptualization of the way that MLB actually plays the game in 2020. If…y'know…MLB plays in 2020. If WAR is going to be our flagship statistic among the *acronymati*, then we need to acknowledge that it contains some old and starting-to-be-out-of-date assumptions about the game. We may need to tinker with it. Here's my idea for how.

—*Russell A. Carleton is an author of Baseball Prospectus.*

Secondhand Sport

by Patrick Dubuque

Back before time stopped, I liked to go to thrift stores. Now that I'm older, I rarely ever buy anything—I don't need much in my life, now—but I still enjoy the old familiar circuit: check to see if there are baseball cards to write about, look for board or card games to play with the kids, scan for random ironic jerseys, hit the book section. It takes ten, maybe fifteen minutes. Thrift stores are the antithesis of modern online shopping, because you don't know what they have, and you don't even really know what you want. It's junk, literal junk, stuff other people thought was worthless. That's what makes it great.

In an idealized economy, thrift stores shouldn't exist. Everybody has a living wage, and every product has a durability that exactly matches its desired life; nothing should need to be given away, no one should need to be given to. But then, thrift stores shouldn't work on a customer experience level, either. You wouldn't think an ethos of "let's make everything disorganized and hard to find" would lead to customer satisfaction, but low-budget retailers like TJ Maxx and Ross thrive on this model. People like bargain hunting as much for the hunting as the bargain; it's part of the experience, spending time as if it's a wager. There's a thrill, occasionally, in inefficiency.

In sports, the modern overuse of the word "inefficiency" is a condemnation: It insinuates that there is *an* efficiency, a correct way to be found, and that all other ways are wrong ways. It's prevalent in baseball but hardly contained to it; the lifehack, the Silicon Valley disruption are other examples of productivity creep in our daily lives. Their modern success makes plenty of sense. Maximization of resources, after all, is its own puzzle, and an industry of European board games is founded upon it. It's fun to take a system and optimize it, unravel it like a sudoku puzzle. If there's only one kind of genius, after all, there's no way anyone can fail to appreciate it.

Baseball has been hacking away at these perceived inefficiencies since its inception: platoons, bullpens, farm systems were all installed to extract more out of the tools at hand. But it's been a particular badge of the sabermetric movement, from Ken Phelps and his All-Star Team to Ricardo Rincon and the darlings of *Moneyball*. It's business, but it's also an ethos: the idea that there's treasure among the trash, something we all failed to appreciate until someone brought it to light.

It's the myth that made Sidd Finch so enticing, that fuels so many "best shape" narratives and new pitch promises. We all, athletes and unathletic sportswriters, want to believe that there's genius trapped inside us, and that it's just a matter of puzzling out the combination to unlock it. That our art, our style is the next inefficiency, waiting for our own Billy Beane. It's why we root for underdogs, and why we're excited for the Mike Tauchmans and the Eurubiel Durazos, champions of skin-deep mediocrity.

Except we aren't anymore, really. The days of "Free X" have descended beyond the ring of irony and into obscurity. There are still Xs to be freed, or at least one X, duplicated endlessly: Mike Ford, Luke Voit, Max Muncy. The undervalued one-dimensional slugger demonstrated how the game hasn't quite culturally caught up to its logical extreme. But for those who don't fit the rather spacious mold, times are grimmer. As Rob Arthur revealed several months ago, there's been a marked increase in the number of sub-replacement relievers. It's the outcome of a greater number of teams forced to play out games without the talent to win them, but it's also emblematic of the modern tendency of teams to dispose of their disposable assets, burning through cost-controlled arms the way that man chopped down forests in *The Lorax*. Stuff just isn't built to outlive their original owners anymore.

It's unsurprising, given how well-mined the market for inefficiencies has been of late. The disciples of the early analytics departments, and the disciples of those, have proliferated the league, with only a few backwater holdouts. The league has grown smarter, but every team has learned the same lesson. In fact, the phenomenon creates a peculiar kind of feedback loop: As teams value a specific subset of players or skills, prospective athletes learn to increase their own marketability by conforming themselves to the demands of their prospective employers.

And that's tragic, in the way that the extinction of animals is tragic; a certain amount of biodiversity in baseball has been lost. Shortstops hit like outfielders. Pitchers don't hit at all. Only the catchers remain idiosyncratic, thanks to the defensive demands of their position; eventually they too will be required to produce like everyone else, or they'll meet the fate of their battery mates. A perfect economy requires perfect production.

I mentioned earlier that more and more, I leave thrift stores empty-handed. It is true that I am more discerning than in the past; my bookshelves are full, and there are more streaming films than I will ever be able to watch. But there are other factors at play.

Thrift stores are, in a way, the bond markets of retail. When the economy is rough and other retailers are struggling, more people look secondhand for their products. But as recently as last year, publications were noting a reversal of the trend: Companies like Goodwill and Savers were expanding despite a strong economy. Publications credited a heightened sense of environmentalism and a rejection of cutting-edge fashion as drivers behind the increase, though the more likely answer is the modern American economy hasn't showered its favors equally, particularly among the young.

But it is more than just the economy. Baseball and thrift stores share something else in common, evident in our current conversations about re-starting the sport: They live in the gray area between public service and private enterprise. Thrift stores provide affordable necessities to lower-class citizens, and collectibles and fashion for the middle-class. Because of the success of the latter, prices have gone up across the board. Especially in terms of clothing, the middle-class flight from fashion into vintage has instead carried the aftereffects of fashion, including its costs, into a territory where people just want clothes. But there's another factor in the rise of prices, in the form of the internet.

The Goodwills of the world have grown smarter, too, employing the internet to extract full value from their detritus. Ebay, similarly, has lost much of the charm it had as a new frontier around the turn of the century. Everything has a price point now; even individual taste is no match for the algorithm, because anything rare, no matter how niche its market, is a collectible to someone.

The internet has had the same effect on thrift stores that sabermetrics has had on baseball; its equivalent to OBP was the bar scanner. As detailed in Slate, the rise of second-party stores on eBay and Amazon birthed an entire industry of used-good salespeople, armed with PDAs and scanners, buying books for three dollars to sell online for five. The author, Michael Savitz, reports earning $60,000 by working nearly 80 hours a week; he makes it clear that this is not a vocation of his choosing. It's long hours, with no real creativity or individuality, skimming the cream off of a local establishment and flipping it to someone with a little more money on the other side of the country. And once the vocation exists, the obvious question arises: why wait to put the wares out on the shelves? Why allow value to exist at all?

Nothing is ruined. Thrift stores will continue to sell polo shirts and DVDs, and baseball will continue to exist and make or lose money, depending on who you believe. But as we continue to refine our knowledge, we lose something in the conquest for efficiency, a delight born out of the unknown. The problem isn't the efficiency itself; we can't blame the booksellers, or the people sweeping freeways to collect grams of platinum from damaged catalytic converters. The problem is a system that requires this sort of profit-skimming behavior in order to feed families (or, for corporations, maximize shareholder return).

Miami Marlins 2021

In times like these, with the 2020 season on the brink and the collective bargaining agreement close behind, it can often feel like the current situation is untenable. It can't keep going like this, even if we don't know what to do about it. But as with thrift stores, there's an equally irresistible feeling that it *has* to keep going, that it would be unimaginable to not have this broken, amazing sport. Both industries exist on an invisible foundation of friction, of chaos and unpredictability, even as both see their foundations buffed down to a perfect, untouchable polish. But if COVID-19 and its financial ramifications do, as some have suggested, make it such that the baseball that returns is fundamentally different than the baseball that came before, perhaps this is the time to lean in, and change the game even more. Fix bunting. Make defense more difficult. Create viable, alternate strategies. Add some chaos back into baseball. It's fun when no one knows quite where things are. ■

—*Patrick Dubuque is an author of Baseball Prospectus.*

Steve Dalkowski Dreaming

by Steven Goldman

We dream of being a pitcher, of starring in the major leagues. Depending on your age and your sense of historical perspective, you might imagine yourself as Walter Johnson, throwing harder than anyone else—hitting more batters than anyone else, too, but always feeling bad about it. You could picture yourself as a Tom Seaver or a David Cone, with all the stuff in the world but still being cerebral about it, thinking about so much more than burning 'em in there. There are so many models one could choose: You could be a Lefty Gomez, Jim Bouton, or Bill Lee, skilled, but not taking the whole thing too seriously, or a Lefty Grove, Bob Gibson, or Steve Carlton, powerful but treating each start like a mission to be survived instead of a game to be enjoyed.

Very few would dream of being Steve Dalkowski, the former Baltimore Orioles prospect who died of COVID-19 last week at the age of 80. Yet, there is something just as noble in Dalkowski's negative accomplishments—and accomplishments is what they are—as there is in the precision-engineered pitching of a Greg Maddux. You have to be very good to be that bad. Dalkowski had all of the stuff of the greatest pitchers but none of the command; his story is not one of failing to conquer his limitations, but striving against one of the cruelest hands that fate or genetics or personality can deal us: A desire to achieve great things which is almost but not quite matched by the ability to meet that goal.

As with Johnson, Grove, Bob Feller, and the rest of the hard-throwing pitchers who played before the advent of modern radar guns, we have to take the word of the players and coaches who saw Dalkowski pitch as to his velocity. He was a hard-drinking, maximum-effort pitcher who, if their memories are to be believed, consistently threw over 100 miles per hour. His was the Maltese Fastball, the stuff that dreams are made of. The problem is that velocity without command and control is still a good distance from utility. Dalkowski was the most effective towel you could design for a fish, the sleekest bathing suit intended to be worn by an astronaut, but that doesn't mean he wasn't beautiful: We can appreciate a journey even if it doesn't end at the intended destination.

Whether because of sloppy mechanics he couldn't calm, an inability to understand that a consistent 98 in the strike zone would likely be more effective than a consistent 110 out of it, or all that beer, Dalkowski could never make the adjustments that pitchers like Feller and Nolan Ryan made before him, possibly because he had so far to go: Feller, who never pitched in the minors, came up at 17 and spent three years walking almost seven batters per nine innings before settling in at 3.8 beginning when he was 20. Ryan started out walking over six batters per nine but gradually improved as his long career played out; for him to go from 6.2 walks per nine with the 1966 Greenville Mets to 3.7 with the 1989 Texas Rangers represents a 40 percent reduction. An equivalent improvement by Dalkowski would still have left him walking over 11 batters per nine innings.

Dalkowski was like *The Room* of pitchers, a player so bad he became good again. Cal Ripken, Sr., who both played with and managed Dalkowski, recalled in a 1979 *Sporting News* "where are they now" piece the occasion when the pitcher crossed up his catcher and his fastball, "hit the plate umpire smack in the mask. The mask broke all to pieces and the umpire wound up in the hospital for three days with a concussion. If they ever had a radar gun in those days, I'll bet Dalkowski would have been timed at 110 miles an hour."

Signed by the Orioles out of New Britain High in Connecticut in 1957, Dalkowski was sent to Kingsport in the Appalachian League, where he pitched 62 innings. He allowed only 22 hits in 62 innings, or 3.2 per nine, a number with no equivalent in major league history (though Aroldis Chapman came close in 2014), and also struck out 121 (17.6 per nine) and walked 129 (18.7). He was also charged with 39 wild pitches. That June, one of his fastballs clipped a Dodgers prospect named Bob Beavers and carried away part of his ear. "The first pitch was over the backstop, the second pitch was called a strike, I didn't think it was," Beavers said last year. "The third pitch hit me and knocked me out, so I don't remember much after that. I couldn't get in the sun for a while, and I never did play baseball again." Former minor leaguer Ron Shelton based the *Bull Durham* pitcher Nuke LaLoosh on Dalkowski. And yet, to see him as a figure of fun, an amusing loser, is to misunderstand something unique and strange.

Dalkowski kept on posting some of the strangest lines in baseball history. Pitching for the Stockton Ports of the Class C California League in 1960, he struck out 262 and walked 262 in 170 innings. Yet, he did improve, especially after pitching for Earl Weaver at Elmira in 1962. Weaver had previously had Dalkowski at Aberdeen in 1959, but wasn't ready to grapple with him then. This time he was. "I had grown more and more concerned about players with great physical abilities who could not learn to correct certain basic deficiencies no matter how much you instructed or drilled them," he related in his autobiography, *It's What You Learn After You Know It All That Counts*. He got permission from the Orioles to give all of his players the Stanford-Binet IQ test. "Dalkowski finished in the 1 percentile in his ability to understand facts. Steve, it was said to say, had the ability to do everything but learn." [sic]

IQ tests are problematic diagnostic tools, so take Weaver's estimate of Dalkowski's mental capabilities with a grain of salt. What's important is that even if he got to the right answer by way of the wrong reason, Weaver had learned something valuable. His insight was to stop asking Dalkowski to learn new pitches and just let him get by with the two that he had. Were Dalkowski a prospect today, that would have been a no-brainer: Can't develop a third pitch? The bullpen is right over there, sir. Player development wasn't like that then, but Weaver, temporarily Dalkowski's mentor, could let him work with what he had. According to Weaver, the pitcher responded: "In the final 57 innings he pitched that season Dalkowski gave up 1 earned run, struck out 110 batters, and walked only 11." It's not true—as per the *Elmira Star-Gazette*, as of late July, Dalkowski had walked 71 in 106 innings and finished with 114 in 160 innings, which means Dalkowski's control actually faded at the end of the season rather than improved—but that doesn't mean it didn't happen in some sense, just that it didn't happen that way. Again, it's the journey, not the destination, and his ERA was 3.04 so *something* had gone right.

Also along the way: The next spring, Orioles manager Billy Hitchcock was rooting for Dalkowski to make the team as a long-man—maybe Weaver had gotten through to him. There were things out of Weaver's control, like the universe's twisted sense of humor: that March, Dalkowski's elbow went "twang."

You sometimes read that it was the Orioles' insistence on Dalkowski learning the curve that did him in, but even if they hadn't learned their lesson, the injury was probably just a coincidence: Dalkowski had thrown an incredible number of pitches over the previous few years. Still, it testifies to the dangers of trying to get what you want and risking the loss of what you had. Dalkowski tried to come back, but the 110-mph stuff was gone. A pitcher with no control and no stuff is…a civilian. What followed were years of vagabond living, arrests for drunkenness. There were Alcoholics Anonymous meetings, assistance from baseball alumni associations, but none of it took. From the 1990s until the time of his passing he dwelt in an assisted living facility, suffering from alcohol-related dementia. He'd been a heavy drinker since his teenage years. As with all those pitches per game, there was a price to be paid. You make choices on the journey and some of them are irrevocable. It's like a fairy tale: "Bite of poison apple? Don't mind if I do."

In the aforementioned *Sporting News* profile, Chuck Stevens, the head of the Association of Professional Ballplayers of America, a ballplayer charity, said, "I've got nothing against drinking. I do it myself sometimes. But, I don't condone common drunkenness. We went through lots of heartache and many dollars, but Dalkowski didn't want to help himself and we weren't going to keep him drunk." The journey is *un*like a fairy tale: No one will come along and kiss it better, not if they're busy forming judgments.

In the end, we are left with a sort of philosophical chicken/egg conundrum: Is failing to meet your goals evidence of unfulfilled potential or the lack of it? Isn't what you did by definition what you were capable of doing? Or could you have broken through to something better with the right help, the right lucky break? These are unanswerable questions, and how we try to answer them may say more about us than about the people we're judging.

No pitcher ever has it easy. *All* pitchers must work hard. *All* pitchers must refine their craft. It's almost never just about *stuff*. Dalkowski dreaming is no insult to the great pitchers who made it; from Pete Alexander to Max Scherzer, they have all earned their way up. And yet, if it is true that we can only do as much as we can do, then the journey would be more of an adventure, the ultimate triumph or defeat more noble, if like Dalkowski we lacked 100 percent of the confidence, the command, the self-possession, the commitment, the resistance to making bad decisions that so many great players possess—to be gloriously human. Or, to put it more succinctly, it would be fun to be able to throw as hard as any person ever has. Even if just for a moment, and even if nothing more came of it than that, no one could say you hadn't lived life to the fullest.

—*Steven Goldman is an author of Baseball Prospectus.*

A Reward For A Functioning Society

by Cory Frontin and Craig Goldstein

On July 5, Nationals reliever Sean Doolittle said in the middle of a press conference regarding the restart of Major League Baseball and what would later be known as summer camp, "sports are like the reward of a functioning society." This sentence was amidst a much longer, thoughtful reply about the societal and health conditions under which MLB players were being brought back. It's a very similar sentiment to one Jane McManus used on April 7, when she discussed the White House's meeting with sports commissioners. She said "sports are the effect of a functioning society—not the precursor."

Both versions of the same sentiment spoke to a laudable ideal in the context of a country that was not addressing a rampaging virus, and opting instead to bring sports back for the feeling of normalcy rather than the reality of it. "Priorities," as McManus said.

On Wednesday, the NBA's Milwaukee Bucks conducted a wildcat/political strike, refusing to come out for Game 5 of their playoff series against the Orlando Magic. The Magic refused to accept the forfeit, and shortly thereafter other playoff series were threatened by player strikes. Eventually the league moved to postpone that day's games, folding to players leveraging their united power.

The backdrop against which these actions took place was the shooting by police of Jacob Blake. Blake was shot in the back seven times by police, as he attempted to get into his vehicle. He managed to survive the assault, but is paralyzed from the waist down.

⚾ ⚾ ⚾

The step taken to walk out, first by the Milwaukee Bucks, then subsequently by other NBA, WNBA, and MLB teams, was a step toward upholding the virtue of the sentiment described by McManus and Doolittle. But that sentiment does not align with the broad history of sports in this and other countries, a history that contradicts the core of the idealistic statement.

Sports have been a significant part of American society for most of its existence, expanding in importance and influence in recent years. The idea that society was functioning in a way that was worthy of the reward of sports for most of that time is laughable. Much of America is not functioning and has not functioned for Black people, full stop. The oppressed people at the center of this political act by players, specifically Black players, in concert throughout the NBA and in fits and starts throughout Major League Baseball, have not known a society that functions for them rather than *because* of them.

Politics has been part of the sports landscape since the inception of sport, but for just about as long people have bemoaned its presence. Sports are to be an escape, it is said. An escape from what, though? A functioning society?

No, the presence of sports has never signified a cultural or political system that is on the up and up. Rather, the presence of sports *reflect and reinforce the society that produces them.*

⚾   ⚾   ⚾

The Negro Leagues were born out of societal dysfunction. The need for entirely separate leagues, composed of Black and Latino players barred from the Major Leagues because of racism? That is not a functioning society, and yet there were sports.

Even the integration of players from the Negro Leagues resulted in a transfer of power and wealth from Black-owned businesses and communities and into white ones, mirroring the dysfunction that had bled into every aspect of American society at the time. Japheth Knopp noted in the Spring 2016 Baseball Research Journal:

> *The manner in which integration in baseball—and in American businesses generally—occurred was not the only model which was possible. It was likely not even the best approach available, but rather served the needs of those in already privileged positions who were able to control not only the manner in which desegregation occurred, but the public perception of it as well in order to exploit the situation for financial gain. Indeed, the very word integration may not be the most applicable in this context because what actually transpired was not so much the fair and equitable combination of two subcultures into one equal and more homogenous group, but rather the reluctant allowance—under certain preconditions—for African Americans to be assimilated into white society.*

To understand the value of a movement, though, is not to understand how it is co-opted by ownership, but to know the people it brings together and what they demand. When Jackie Robinson—the player who demarcated the inevitability of the end of the Negro leagues—attended the March on Washington for Jobs and Freedom in 1963, he did so with his family and marched alongside the people. He stood alongside hundreds of thousands to fight for their common civil and labor rights. "The moral arc of the universe is long," many freedom fighters have echoed, "but it bends towards justice." The bend, it is less frequently said, happens when a great mass of people place the moral arc of the universe on their knee and apply force, as Jackie, his family, and thousands of others did that day.

⚾ ⚾ ⚾

Of course, taking the moral arc of the universe down from the mantle and bending it is not without risk. Perhaps the outsized influence of athletes is itself a mark of a dysfunctional society, but, nonetheless, hundreds of athletes woke up on Wednesday morning with the power to bring in millions of dollars in revenues. That very power, as we would come to find out, was matched with the equal and opposite power to *not* bring those revenues. That power, in hands ranging from the Milwaukee Bucks, to Kenny Smith in the *Inside the NBA* Studio, from the unexpected ally, Josh Hader, and his largely white teammates to the notably Black Seattle Mariners, would be exercised for a single demand: the end to state violence against Black people. Not unlike the March itself, it sat at the intersection of the civil rights of Black Americans and bold labor action. The March on Washington stood in the face of a false notion of integration—against an integration of extraction but not one of equality—and proposed something different. Just the same, the acts of solidarity of August 26, 2020 will be remembered in stark defiance of MLB's BLM-branded, but ultimately empty displays on opening weekend.

Bold defiance like this can never be without risk. By choosing to exercise this power, the Milwaukee Bucks took a risk. They risked vitriol and backlash from those they disagreed with. They risked fines or seeing their contracts voided, as a walkout like this is prohibited by their CBA. They risked forfeiting a playoff game, one that, as the No. 1 seed in the playoffs, they'd worked all year to attain. They didn't know how Orlando would respond. It wasn't clear that other teams throughout the league would follow suit in solidarity. And it wasn't known the league would accept these actions and moderately co-opt them by "postponing" games that would have featured no players.

If the league reschedules the games, some of the athletes' risk—their shared sacrifice—will be diminished, in retrospect. But they did not know any of that when they took that risk. And it is often left to athletes to take these risks when others in society won't, especially those of their same socioeconomic status and levels of influence.

It is athletes, specifically BIPOC athletes, that take them, though, because they live with the risk of being something other than white in this country every day. They are no strangers to the realities of police brutality. It seems incongruous then, to say that sports are a reward for a functioning society when we rely on athletes to lead us closer to being a functioning society. Luckily, our beloved athletes, WNBA players first and foremost among them, understand what sports truly are: a pipebender for the moral arc of the universe.

—Craig Goldstein is editor in chief of Baseball Prospectus. Cory Frontin is an author of Baseball Prospectus.

Index of Names

Aguilar, Jesús 16
Alcantara, Sandy 42
Alfaro, Jorge 18
Alvarez, Eddy 74
Anderson, Brian 20
Bass, Anthony 44
Berti, Jon 22
Bleday, JJ 74, 90
Bleier, Richard 46
Boxberger, Brad 48
Brigham, Jeff 83
Brinson, Lewis 24
Burdick, Peyton 96
Cabrera, Edward 84, 91
Castano, Daniel 50
Cervelli, Francisco 26
Chisholm, Jazz 28, 92
Cimber, Adam 52
Conine, Griffin 75
Cooper, Garrett 30
Detwiler, Ross 54
Devers, Jose 76, 98
Díaz, Isan 77
Diaz, Lewin 78, 97
Dickerson, Corey 32
Encarnación, Jerar 78
Floro, Dylan 56

Fulton, Dax 85, 95
García, Yimi 58
Garrett, Braxton 85, 97
Guzman, Jorge 86
Harrison, Monte 79
Hernandez, Elieser 60
Hoyt, James 62
Johnson, Osiris 98
Leibrandt, Brandon 86
León, Sandy 80
López, Pablo 64
Marte, Starling 34
Meyer, Max 87, 91
Misner, Kameron 81, 97
Neidert, Nick 66
Nunez, Nasim 95
Ramirez, Harold 81
Rogers, Trevor 68, 93
Rojas, Miguel 36
Rucinski, Drew 87
Sanchez, Jesus 82, 94
Sanchez, Sixto 70, 89
Scott, Connor 83, 98
Sierra, Magneuris 38
Smith, Josh A. 72
Smith, Josh D. 88
Wallach, Chad 40

For the Joy of Keeping Score

THIRTY81 Project is an ongoing graphic design project focused on the ballparks of baseball. Since being established in 2013, scorecards have been a fundemantal part of the effort. Each two-page card is uniquely ballpark-centric — there are 30 variants — and designed with both beginning and veteran scorekeepers in mind. Evolving over the years with suggestions from fans, broadcasters, and official scorers, the sheets are freely available to everyone as printable letter-size PDFs at the project webshop: www.THIRTY81Project.com

Download, Print, Score, Repeat …

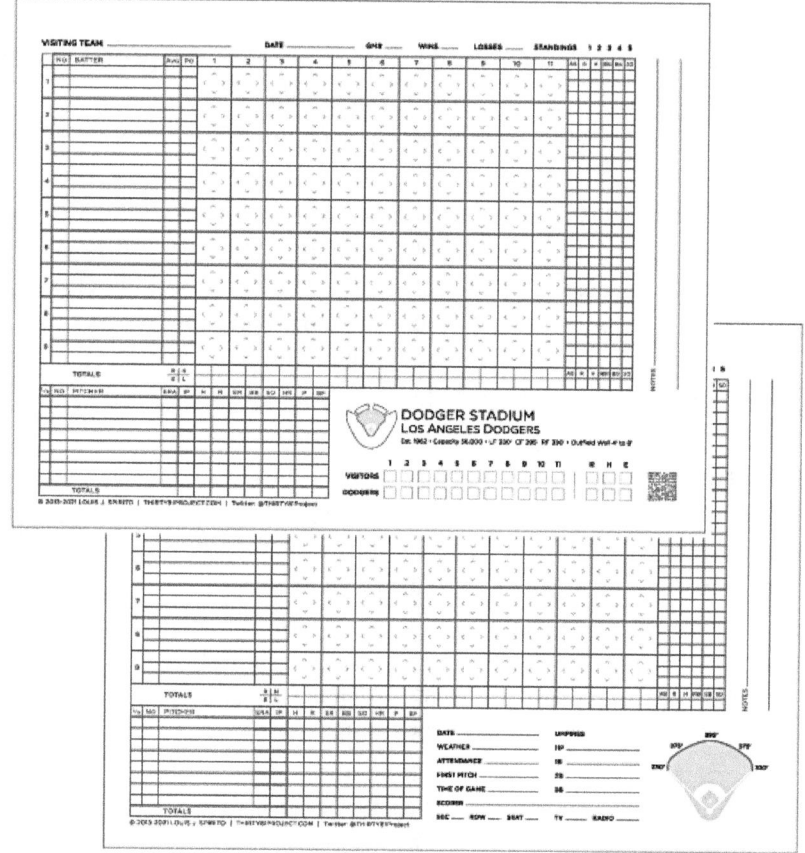

Scorecard design ©2013-2021 Louis J. Spirito | THIRTY81Project